TRANSFORMING YOUR
OFFICE

TRANSFORMING YOUR
OFFICE

Leslie Capek

[signature: Leslie Capek]

and books

South Bend, Indiana

TRANSFORMING YOUR OFFICE
Copyright © 1981 by Leslie Capek

All rights reserved. No part of this book may be reproduced or transmitted in any form or by any means, electronic or mechanical, including photocopying, recording or by any information storage and retrieval system, without permission in writing from the publisher.

and books
702 South Michigan, South Bend, Indiana 46618

ISBN: 0-89708-080-7
Library of Congress Catalog Card Number: 81-68395

First printing, December, 1981

Printed in the United States of America

Additional copies available:

the distributors
702 South Michigan
South Bend, IN 46618

For my siblings, Michael Alan, Wendy Jean and Christine Elizabeth.

PREFACE

Leslie Capek is a talented young architect now practicing in the Midwest. A graduate of Yale, she received her Master of Architecture from the University of Illinois, where she pursued the research on principles of office design that led to this book. Her comprehensive and uninhibited approach is a unique contribution for a time when the value and role of work in our society are being seriously questioned. Her book is as far ranging, imaginative, stimulating, and perplexing as the author herself.

                        Robert B. Riley, AIA
                        Head and Professor
                        Department of Landscape Architecture
                        University of Illinois at Urbana-Champaign
                        July, 1981

ACKNOWLEDGEMENTS

Not surprisingly, this book took twice as much time and effort as I had first anticipated. The help and encouragement of many people was a critical element in the final product. Besides all of my friends and relatives, several people deserve special recognition:

Mary Ramos
Robert B. Riley
Zorine Radovich

Thomas F. Lyon
Kathy A. Robinson
Dennis R. Humphries

CONTENTS

FOREWORD xi
ONE: PROCESS
    Problems of Productivity 17
    Patterns of Promise 27
    States of Mind 35
    Work is Fantasy 39
    Work is Memory 41
    Work is Daydream 44
    Work is Creativity 51
    Work is Ritual 57
    Work is Play 61
TWO: POWER
    People 69
    The Individual 79
    The Team 84
    The Organization 89
    Information 97
    Servants 101
    Muses 116
    Paraphernalia 121
    Things as a Whole 123
THREE: PLACE
    Models, Symbols and Attributes 129
    Location 139
    Form 151
    Image 165
EPILOGUE 183
NOTES 185
BIBLIOGRAPHY 193

"The traditional building forms long ago invested with meaning have been important to mankind because they accomodated the initial act of constructing a dwelling, the first tangible boundary beyond the body...calling attention to the sources of human energy and to our place between heaven and earth..."
— Kent C. Bloomer and Charles W. Moore

"Far better it is to dare mighty things, to win glorious triumphs, even though checkered with failure, than to take rank with those poor spirits who neither enjoy nor suffer much, because they live in the grey twilight that knows not victory or defeat."
— Theodore Roosevelt

FOREWORD

What do Johnny Carson and J.R. Ewing, your local banker and insurance agent have in common? They do their work sitting behind a desk and chances are that you do too. The office a place where an increasing percentage of the American work force spends forty hours a week, more or less. By the year 2000, half of the American work force will be office employees.

Trends born in the Industrial Revolution of the late 19th century led to an accumulation of one billion square feet of office space in America by 1930. Despite the Great Depression and the Second World War, this figure doubled to two billion square feet of office space by 1960. From 1970 to 1973, construction of an additional 500 million square feet of office space was started. Construction tapered off in the mid-1970's, due to the mild recession, then made up for lost time in the close of the decade. In the 1980's, building booms hit almost every major urban center, in spite of climbing interest rates.

The futurists predict, however, that someday everyone will be working in home offices with the aid of cable connected, computerized information systems. That day is still very far away. For this generation and at least the next two, the office is here to stay.

Originally located in city centers, offices joined the suburban exodus in the 1950's and are now found in even the most rural locations. One of the first large corporations to move out of the city was General Foods. Planning efforts began as early as 1937. By 1949 General Foods had spilled out of its main offices at 250 Park Avenue to other spaces in midtown Manhattan. General urban congestion and high operating costs were the main reasons for leaving the city. On May 1, 1950, the committee, which had surveyed possible new locations in other cities, as well as in Brooklyn, Queens and the suburban area around New York, recommended White Plains. The community was close enough to Manhattan to make it accessible, yet suburban enough to offer a campus-like setting with the advantages of clean air, open space and green surroundings. General Foods received a zoning variance to build in the residential area, but they also received a restriction on the height of their new building. The firm made an additional effort to prevent an intrusion in the environment by planning a thorough landscaping program to screen the complex. Months of careful planning prepared the firm to move 1300 employees and 18,000 pieces of office equipment over three weekends in April of 1954.

No matter how the world of business changes, a better office will always have a competitive edge. Someday the quality of the office both as a marketing image and a working environment may be appreciated by accounting standards as an intangible asset, worth much more than the combination of real estate, construction, furniture and equipment costs. The value of the office on the corporate books should reflect its ultimate impact on total productivity, just as if it were some

rare form of customized machinery

which in fact, it really is. The office must be understood as both the container and its contents. Careful coordination and balance between the office as a place and a process is a vital ingredient for individual as well as corporate success.

A subtitle for this broad look at an important aspect of modern life might be the "how and why wonder-book of offices..." The emphasis is on the close relation between everything from electronic information systems, the design of desks and work stations, and the shape of the office buildings to the ways people use their brains, or don't use them, as the case may be. The wide range of topics suggested by these interrelated factors has required an interdisciplinary approach to the subject. Data has been drawn from the areas of psychology, sociology, organization and information theory, architecture, furniture and product design, philosophy and cultural anthropology. Resources included conversations with others, books, manuscripts, magazine and newspaper articles, and television programs, in addition to my personal experiences as an architectural designer in developing offices, and first-hand observations as a direct participant in a wide range of office environments.

The format of this book groups the many facts and concepts into three basic sections: Process, Power and Place. The discussions combine down-to-earth practicalities with more theoretical analysis. The section on Process is a detailed look at what happens inside the office and what happens inside the individual who is in the office. The section on Power deals with the sources and structure of energy applied to the principle office task of organizing information. This section focuses on the characteristics of people, teams and organizations, and how they are served by office equipment, furnishings and accessories. The final section on Place discusses the architecture of offices. The emphasis is on the range of options available for creating an office that is architecturally in tune with any particular organization. Basic architectural concepts are also explained to help the reader reach increased awareness and enjoyment of the daily spatial experience encountered at work.

This book is unique because it brings together in detail a combination of ideas which have generally been treated separately by other authors. There is certainly much more information concerning each particular subject touched on by this text, but the purpose here has been to develop a well-rounded understanding of the office from as many angles as possible. The illustrations and quotations are intended to remind the reader to apply each successive concept back to a growing perception of the office as a whole.

This book coordinates the basic issues and aspects of what the office is, ways it may be improved and why changes are necessary to meet the business challenges of the future. The presentation includes ideas and methods which any individual can use to increase personal productivity. To get the most out of the office, it must be seen as both the support and inspiration for business activities. Office life can be a much richer experience than most people imagine. This book suggests many of the reasons why.

Just as a doctor's responsibility includes promoting the general health, so the architect's responsibility includes helping people

"to explore sensitivities to place."

Architects are also responsible for helping people learn to manipulate the environments in which they live and work in order to satisfy their personal needs; knowing how to use and enjoy the habitat is something most people take for granted.

Certainly, everyone has a vested interest in the environment in which one lives and works. As each person develops a better understanding of how that environment functions, that person will be able to make a more significant contribution to the creation of that environment and its subsequent modifications to meet the changing requirements of both the individual and the society of which one is a part.

ONE
PROCESS

PROCESS:
Problems of Productivity

In the search for success, every office is ultimately unique. Yet the basis for understanding any particular office must begin with an examination of the things or principles which many offices seem to share. If the roots of successful office operation lie in the contributions of individual people, then the common problem of individual productivity is of prime concern. Statisticians claim that "office productivity has climbed a bare 4% in the past decade."[1] This issue will be the focus of our exploration of the office in terms of personal, interpersonal and physical factors. In all cases, it is important to remember that taking advantage of an opportunity and solving a problem are usually just opposite sides of the coin. These situations can grow from present conditions or they can derive from conditions of the future, which often seems to arrive long before we are prepared.

An obvious source of future problems and opportunities is the rapid change of technology, which can trigger a chain reaction that penetrates every aspect of office life. The advent of computerized word processing equipment, for example, "will challenge all the old executive turfs, the hierarchies, the sexual role divisions, and the departmental barriers of the past."[2] Some analysists predict that millions of secretarial jobs may disappear as survival-minded businesses continue to pickup on new systems. Advocates of the information industries claim that "for those who can adapt, the secretary will rise to the role of paraprincipal; sharing in some of the professional work..."[3] One can at least expect to see an expansion of the secretary's primary responsibility for helping the executive seek out and digest the increasing quantity of data necessary for making informed decisions.

As new office technology increases the flow of information, many offices respond by decentralizing. Observers point to the growing shift towards multiple command systems and matrix organizations. In such offices,"the network is not 'coordinated' by anybody; the participating bodies coordinate themselves so that one may speak of 'auto-coordination'."[4] In these circumstances office workers must be cooperative, creative problem solvers more than ever before. As office operations increase in complexity, more workers are needed "who seek meaning, who question authority...who accept responsibility, who are less pre-programmed and faster on their feet."[5] The password of the successful office of the future might be zero-based thinking, a jargon expression which simply means openmindedness and flexibility.

Office personnel at every level may suffer anxiety and frustration at the thought of future uncertainties. They are quick to blame advancing technology and an unstable economy as the source of their problems. Yet many expectations are actually misconceptions. Researchers predict that with the current advance of technology "work grows less, not more repetitive." Especially in the office, "each person (will be) doing a somewhat larger, rather than smaller task."[6] Contrary to popular belief, the general facts show that as investments in new technology increase, so does the creation of new jobs. Whether or not one is prepared for the changes determines if they will present a problem or an opportunity.

"We will see a sharp division between those white-collar workers who move up to more responsible positions and those who move down and eventually out."[7]

The organization as a whole, as well as the individual, is faced with a critical imperative to adapt to the swiftly changing conditions of office life. Inflexible organizations can get caught in a deadly squeeze between the complexity of business situations and the need for faster and more accurate decision-making. The crisis faced by the office today is not unlike the one faced in the days of Alexander Graham Bell, when firms that failed to subscribe to telephone service were often, and quite rapidly, left far behind in the resulting commercial dust.

The inertia of outdated office operations poses a serious threat to any firm's chances for survival and growth. "Just because something exists doesn't mean it should be preserved."[8]

The prospect of significant change to traditional office procedures can seem quite impossible when they have become the deeply habituated infrastructure of office life. The costs of adaptation are often much more than the expense of new hardware. When changes are first introduced, the resulting temporary inefficiencies come into immediate conflict with the constant demands of the daily production routine. This in turn can waste time and energy, and create interpersonal tensions until people become familiar with the new system.

Though the costs of office adaptation may appear insurmountable, it is folly to think the alternatives any more economical. In the long run, there are no alternatives to accepting the inevitable evolution of human society. Yet the first steps which an organization takes towards accomodating new circumstances most often begin with the perceptions and suggestions of specific individuals.

Whether changes might be initiated from the "top" or the "bottom" of an organization, they are often deterred by a fear of "rocking the boat". The president may find it easier to hang onto the status quo until his retirement than incur the displeasure of the board of directors when the costs of proposed changes are figured into the annual financial statements. The secretary may find running back-and-forth from the Xerox machine in the file room to the switchboard at her desk is far simpler than to ask the boss to install a second phone. This unfortunate attitude is maintained in the face of problems/opportunities of the present as well as the future.

Many of the present situations in the office which create annoyance, frustration and unhappiness are so widespread and have been criticized for so long that we almost take them for granted or accept them as inevitable and unchangeable. There seems to be a perpetual series of events that send people home at the end of the day, muttering, "That office is so messed up..." Though these sources of dissatisfaction and low productivity typically exist on personal, interpersonal and physical levels, they are so closely connected with each other that it is often difficult to single out one specific headache from the next.

Personal frustrations within the office are often related to seemingly monotonous work routines, which provide few immediate pleasures and contribute little towards career advancement. There can be a depressing predictability to the endless repetition of typing letters, answering telephones, punching calculators and writing memorandums. The flood of busywork seems to stretch from here to eternity; a dead-end situation that can fill anyone with a sense of futility and helplessness. Obviously, such predicaments are not conducive to energetic efforts and high productivity. Constant states of pressure and overwork can be equally debilitating.

Though such common grievances are typically shared between close associates, most office workers are reluctant to step forward within the organization and tackle the problems openly and constructively, for fear of being labeled a malcontent or a loser. Expressing dissatisfaction with one's position can often be heard as an admission that one's career development is less than satisfactory. Because of the peer pressure of today's office society, there can be a stong taboo against appearing anything less than "totally successful".

On the interpersonal level, all forms of communication inefficiency are a source of frustration and a deterrent to productivity. Searching for misplaced files, waiting for return telephone calls or repeating tasks because of misunderstood instructions are basic examples. The intrigues of office politics and power games can be counter-productive as well. The irritations and lost moments can accumulate over time to wear down the spirit of everyone in the office from the president to the "gofers".

The physical environment of the present day office can be the single biggest source of headaches. Spaces always seem too hot or too cold and the air is either nauseating and stuffy, or else it is blasting so hard out of the diffusers that papers get blown off of desks while people suffer neck cramps and head colds. Clacking typewriters, buzzing fluorescent tubes, noisy conversations, ringing telephones, glaring lights, overflowing files and general visual chaos are enough to drive anyone crazy.

Last but not least among deterrents to productivity is the myth that a legitimate, recognizable office must be occupied by a desk, a credenza, and chair. Such inflexibility can prevent people from tailoring their work environments to serve specific task requirements. The truly useful office should contain the things that help get the job done the best and easiest way, besides conveying an image suitable to the occupant.

Considering the many problems reviewed thus far it isn't surprising that office survival is no small achievement. At times it seems like climbing a mountain, clinging to cracks in the rocks and dodging avalanches. Unless significant changes are effected, the ranks of over-worked, understimulated, unhappy and unproductive office workers will continue to grow. As on international observer has noted,"the office forces the worker's soul to adapt."[9] In his commentary on the world of working in general, author Studs Terkel suggests that, "to survive the day is triumph enough for the walking wounded among the great many of us."[10]

Unfortunately, many people seek to solve these problems with escapism. To think that a 4 day work week or even an 8-hour coffee break might make office life more enjoyable is a delusion. When lives become centered around the rituals of lunch-time or holiday weekends, the potential of every office and its members is wasted. Sometimes the results can be even more devastating. The U.S. Safety Commission has documented that the office worker returning home, especially after happy hour, has become the highest risk on the road.

Is it asking too much, for an office to be less frantic and abrasive or more lively and stimulating than the status quo? Though all the functions that any particular person may perform on the job are indeed necessary, could there not be better modes of office operation which might end the long absence of interest and enjoyment while at the same time promoting efficiency and productivity?

One solution to the problem of personal dissatisfaction may lie in the long overdue resurrection of the work ethic, refocussing energy and intensifying personal involvement in the tasks which occupy most of one's time.

Another solution may be found in the individual's realization that neither he nor she nor anyone else, for that matter, is the axis about which the world turns. Accepting one's lack of absolute control over external events can be the first step toward turning problems into opportunities through adaptation. Learning to see how one's responsibilities dovetail with coworkers, and how these fit together into office operations as a whole can make work both more understandable and more meaningful. A pleasant, exciting work space and a more natural, relaxed, atmosphere might do wonders for the energy level in any office. The payoffs in satisfaction and productivity may well be worth it, if efforts towards these solutions could lead people to rediscover that their daily direct experience of the here and now in the office can be far more pleasurable than they had ever imagined. As Alan Watts suggested, "they must come to their senses for their own personal profit and pleasure."[11] The following scenario outlines some of the possibilities.

Suppose Mary arrives at the office, first as usual. After unlocking the door and turning off the burglar alarm, she may start the coffee or she may not, depending on how busy things will be that day. It doesn't matter, because Bill would just as soon do the coffee himself since he likes to make the first pot a little on the strong side. Joe always comes in about half an hour later because he has to drop his kids off at school. Today is a special day because Mary, Bill and Joe will be putting the final touches on a contract proposal for a big client. They've been working on it for two whole weeks. Mary and Bill are talking about the cover letter for the proposal when they look up in surprise to see Joe rushing in 15 minutes earlier than usual.

"Listen guys," says Joe, "We've got to tie in examples of prior experience related to each aspect of this new job right in the text. We can't do it in a table at the end, because that will be just like what our competitors will be doing, and besides, nobody reads those tables very closely anyway. We've got to hit this client over the head with why we're the best team for the project!"

"Gosh, says Mary, "how much sleep did you get last night?"

"Not too much," says Joe, "this proposal format has really been bugging me and I finally figured out why."

"Now wait a minute," interjects Bill, "It sounds like a nice idea, but how can we do it and still make our printing deadline today?"

"How about this," pipes up Mary, "We each know the proposal and the experience tables backwards and forwards. Let's divide the proposal in three parts, quickly agree on which previous experience item will be assigned where. Then we can split up and each one tackle the re-editing on his own word processor. If we all keep the language simple and basic, there should be no problems with continuity. I think we can do it if we bust ass until lunch time?"

"Okay, Mary," answer Bill and Joe, "besides," they add laughing, "what else can we say, you're the boss."

"Thanks, guys," she answers smiling, "I knew I could always count on you in the clinch—let's go!"

> "If you know how
> to do one thing well,
> you can do everything."[12]

"The only way to 'get the hell out' is to root right in...yes, root right in to where you are." [13]

However unglamourous it may seem, many successful careers began with the individual's persistent efforts to master a simple task, as the key to transforming an apparent trap of monotony into a springboard to success. For the corporate rookie, such prospects might seem less challenging than taking out yesterday's kitchen garbage. One wonders, "why must I limit myself to one thing? Why can't I do anything, or everything?" The catch, of course, is how can anyone appreciate professional standards of performance until one has learned to do at least one thing well? It's not nearly as easy as one might expect. What it takes to do one thing really well can sometimes take a lifetime to understand, let alone accomplish.

Louis Comfort Tiffany was a world renowned artist whose stained glass creations are highly prized by collectors of Art Noveau. His expertise was founded in blind dedication to his craft; the ability to focus on one thing until it was mastered with technical excellence. Likewise, Alexander Graham Bell, John D. Rockefeller and Henry Ford all shared similar talents for singular perseverance, which certainly contributed to the accomplishment of their individual goals. M.C. Escher, the art-techno draftsman, suffered through many years of anonymity. Yet he managed to turn the office drudgery of drafting into aesthetic treasures that bring delight to viewers with wide-ranging tastes. Every serious athlete is familiar with the dictum that "There is no progress without pain." In her popular T.V. series, Mary Tyler Moore has shown how a person can turn the daily obstacle course of the office into a vehicle of growth through sheer persistence, as well as personal charm.

The sociologist, Herbert Marcuse read the danger signals of a "one-dimensional" or shallow existence in the lack of deep involvements with life in a holistic sense. We need to remember that working hard can create a working high, worth enough personal satisfaction to make a salary almost seem like a fringe benefit. Likewise, there are many other focal points for enhancing individual stimulation and productivity at the same time. Many people have hardly begun to realize their potential. Effective teamwork can be a thing of beauty as well as power. There is so much that can be accomplished in any office, especially when people remember there may be a greater purpose hidden in the patterns of the daily exchange.

If such speculation seems a bit unrealistic, one should try to think back to the very first days in the office, when the future appeared as an open, if uncertain, road rather than a moss-covered stone wall.

PROCESS:
Patterns of Promise

The modern specialized office may be the result of slightly over 100 years of evolution, but the origins of organized administration trace back through generations of governments, past the Houses of Parliament, the Palace of Versailles, and the Roman Forum. The unique form of each of these early centers of bureaucracy was developed in direct response to the flow of power and information which were organized there and put to use. The structural nature of each respective government was clearly visible in the architectural expression of the buildings which contained them.

England's Houses of Parliament, built in the 1830's stand as an impressive symbol of order beside the Thames River, in dramatic contrast to the twisted confusion of the surrounding London streets. The structures sheltering the scores of voices which debate the fate of Britannia, are encrusted in countless projections and ornaments which seem to debate each other as well.

The Houses of Parliament physically enclose and visually express the presence of a great many voices, in comparison, the Palace of Versailles was the glorification of a single voice. Built in the countryside outside of Paris during the 1600's the regal estate dominated its entire surroundings. All of the roads from the city and the country converged on the great main gate of the entrance courtyard. Proceeding into the palace one follows the sequence of marble and mirrored halls to ultimately arrive at the inner sanctum, the King's private chamber. This closet was the most private place of the most powerful person in the entire kingdom. This was the place where the king and his advisors, the so-called privvy council, could discuss the most important matters in strictest confidence. U.S. presidential advisors are called "the cabinet" for the same reason.

Where the Palace of Versailles was completely outside of the city and the Houses of Parliament were in the city, but distinct from it, the Roman Forum was totally integrated with the urban center of the ancient Mediterranean world. Little did the Tuscan peasants realize that plazas filled with columns would stand in the fields where they grazed their animals. The columns of the Forum were as noble and eloquent as the senators who debated the issues of the Republic. Just like the columns, the senators were all made of the same stuff, they just stood in different positions relative to one another.

Political power is rooted in the careful management of information and joins rank with religious authority at the dawn of civilization. "We only succeed to the degree that we are well informed."[14]

The people who gathered to celebrate in the sacred circle at Stonehenge didn't know that the priests probably used the giant stones to measure the movements of the sun and the stars from which they could direct the populace when to plant and harvest. The people were led to believe that somehow the priests had magical powers or at least a direct line to the gods. Because the knowledge by which the priests maintained control over society was kept in secret, perhaps it was magic after all.

"A new form always seems to be more or less an absence of form at all, since it is unconsciously judged by reference to consecrated form..."[15]

Any information, captured in pictures, or letters or electronic impulses, is magical and sacred, because the information is, in fact, "the symbolic representation of reality."[16] It is the genie in the bottle, ready to transform itself in an infinite number of ways on command.

The most basic activity of the office today is the collection, storage, recombination and distribution of parcels of information. This is the process of transformation. The trick is to make the changes, the rearrangements, the new groupings in the most beneficial manner. A sort of magic is still a useful ingredient, because the elements of chance are as inescapable as Murphy's Law, the well known idea that anything can go wrong at the worst possible moment. But the "wrongness" of such a catastrophe is determined only by our values and preconceptions regarding the outcome of the project.

More often than not, the things which happen in seeming contrast to our plans can become a gift of chance, presenting opportunities we never imagined. But we have to be on our toes to take the money and run, to make the most of events as they occur. Sensing unexpected opportunities is most difficult because it can require a totally new perspective on one's current involvements. Dropping habitual opinions can be very frightening, like being lost at sea at night without the stars to steer by, until one learns to use the flowing currents of the waters or office events themselves.

"...an accident is perhaps the only thing that really inspires us..."[17]

The activity of handling information in the office can benefit from the inspiring "accidents" of our day to day dealings with each other. Or it may be the office place itself which is inspiring. Facts, such as mailing lists, ideas, such as marketing angles, and feelings, such as personal ambition, each can be energized from the contact between specific work tasks and the flow of office events. When things come together so that they contrast and highlight each other, we may understand them better. For example, when you're listening to Bach and someone switches the station to Dolly Parton, you notice the difference in an immediate, physical and emotional way. But sometimes the comparison alone is not enough to fuse the elements involved in an office task. In this case, the general office environment may provide the force that puts it all together.

How many times has a casual remark made someone look up and say, "hey, that gives me a great idea..."? How many times have the eyes followed a shadow line to find in it the perfect angle for the argument in a letter previously abandoned in confusion. In a way, this book began with an accidental encounter, though a lot of other factors were building up to it and may have led to it eventually in some other form.

The rascal sage of this century, R. Buckminster Fuller, has explained this common but curious phenomenon that others call fate as "the original question-born through occurence of an unexpected interference in experimental interpatternings."[18] The psychologist Singer describes how the flux and flow of people and habitat can invite the sometimes random or spontaneous generation of thoughts: "External stimulus and internal somatic activity compete with the reverberatory associational stream (inner monologue) for attention..." the psychologist Thomkins adds, "The central assembly is at best an untidy aggregate...perpetually vulnerable to interference, drift, disassembly."[19]

Brain functions which are the foundation and analog of all human activities, seem to have powers and abilities beyond the range of personal subjective control. The same sensitive techniques for taking advantage of the brain's spontaneous perceptions and connections could be applied to the management of office activities in many fruitful ways.

The degree to which an office can incorporate chance into its activities and processes may affect productivity. Loosening and opening the networks of information flow may let facts and ideas follow a more natural course, like a river running downhill or electricity charging through a conductor. People who seek the information will find it and use it. Information seems to have a life of its own, to invite use and transformation. Facts used in one office report seem to find their way into other projects. Artificial intelligence can have an effect reaching far beyond the office. The general trend towards small project-oriented teams is one way of optimizing information. The team members may share the same files, tables and telephones as they work together. New inputs are instantly shared.

A less sensitive or controversial strategy for incorporating inspiring chance and productive accidents into the office routine is by increasing the variety and personalization of the work place. Architect Charles Moore's poetic statement sums up the potential: "...habitat should allow the everyday to become exceptional, lead the mind to multiple associations, incorporating changing environments to augment and accent the daily ritual..."[20]

All of this talk about magic and chance as necessary elements of office operation might seem confusing, if not apalling to some people. It is a classic western concept that organizations are founded on the belief that "things are under control-our control." Like the priests and elders of ancient times, today's corporate chiefs and Wall Street wizards have their secret knowledge to help them predict events, to deliver the rain or interest rates or whatever. In Mark Twain's story, the intrepid Yankee made King Arthur's knights believe he could control events, such as a solar eclipse, with the mesmerizing trick of prediction. But exeutive mandates don't make the sun come up every day. In our complex world, events sometimes seem to occur independently of one's efforts to direct them. It may be wiser to accept this reality to a certain extent, rather than deny it with a persistent pretense of being "the top".

Rational ego dreads anything that can loosen its control over individual consciousness. People are wary of the dark side of the moon, often as much as they wonder about it, the unknown, subconscious, irrational elements inside of us all. Daydreaming may be frowned on as a waste of time, which may be a cover-up for the taboo against walking along the edge of an abyss of delusion.

Actually, daydreaming may be a very positive activity, or cognitive phenomenon, according to many psychologists including Jung, Piaget, Perls, Singer and others. Daydreaming may be involved in everything from rehearsal of possible activity, perhaps a presentation for a client, to the play of ideas moved around in the search for associations. In order for such play to fuse ideas and perceptions, the energy and intensity of work must indeed be great. Wishes, goals and dreams can generate such energy when they are supported by the environment. We need to feel special if we are going to do something special. That is why Louis Sullivan, the leading Chicago architect of the 1880's held the ideal "that architecture should carry man from physical or sensual elegance and richness to higher states of transcendent awareness."[21]

Office productivity can increase as individuals develop greater self-awareness of how their personal mental processes fit into work tasks. Similarly, individual work tasks are the components of overall office operations. Many types of processes can be understood at the individual, team and organizational levels. The endless categories of these processes include physical, social, psychological, emotional, and cultural. Yet all of these seem to belong to one of two groups: directed processes versus non-directed processes. This commonly understood dichotomy is also called classic versus romantic, disciplined versus exuberant, Appollo versus Dionysus, or design versus dreams. A deeper awareness of the principles common to many types of processes can help the individual to become a more effective and productive contributor to the office process on all levels.

Two important types of processes are associations and transformations. Associations do not cause fundamental change of the elements involved. As Freud noted,

humor is in the object,

but wit is in the associations. Metaphor, simile, allusion, juxtaposition and disjunction processes are also common to the growth of language and consciousness, besides most artistic and intellectual activities. Language is critically important in the process of the office. Everyone can benefit from a review of the basic elements of grammar and composition.(Composition is actually a dynamic form of association). The level of dynamics displayed in much business correspondence unfortunately is a laughing stock. However, some of the best executed letters are true art forms in their use of language and the subtleties of persuasion. The works of great poets and novelists offer inspiration for those who don't subscribe to the current journals.

An important aspect of composition is the relativity of the elements involved, developed by position, scale, perspective, symbolism, and so on. For example, the artist Marcel Duchamp brought a whole new association and meaning to the common shovel when he put his name on it with the title "In Advance of a Broken Arm" and hung it in a museum. "Visible form often repeated may acquire different meanings with the passage of time and an enduring meaning may be conveyed by different visual forms."[22]

Tranformations differ from associations in that they cause fundamental change of the elements involved. Again, there are both static and dynamic sorts of transformations. The static sorts include:

- ellipse, ellision;

- simplification, reduction, miniaturization, demolition, division;

- complication, intensification, paradox, amplification, duplication, multiplication;

- hyperbole, irony, satire, ridicule, caricature, decadence, demythification, negative distortion;

- dramatize, romanticize, mythification, positive distortion.

Dynamic transformations include the cycles of change and process, of growth and decay, of life. By nature they are both elaborative as well as integrative, unifying as well as ornamental. These principles receive an excellent general discussion in Sullivan's **A System of Architectural Ornament**.

"Parallelism- art science and philosophy fuse as it were into a single vital impulse...the universal power of energy which flows everywhere...seeking expression in form."[23] Thus the energy of change flows from structure to efflorescence.

PROCESS:
States of Mind

---

*"In the pursuit of learning every day something is acquired.
In the pursuit of the Way, every day something is dropped.
Less and less is done until non-action is achieved.
When nothing is done, nothing is left undone.
The world is ruled by letting things take their course.
It cannot be ruled by interfering."*
—*Lao Tsu* [24]

"Growth has its season..."[25] "The time is now..."[26] If mental functions are at the root of office operations, then a better understanding of these functions could put them to more profitable service, for both the individual and the organization.

"Everyman's work shall be manifest: for the day shall declare it because it shall be revealed by fire and the fire shall try everyman's work of what sort it is."[27]

All the processes of man's work, play, creativity or rituals originate in the phenomena of patterned behavior, which is based in the reptillian core of the brain structure. The R-complex is a more primitive element of the brain than the complexly folded cortex layers which evolved at a later stage, along with conscious thought. As a result the neurological, biological and even cosmic process are matched, head to head. In one head, observations made consciously are processed while in the other, observations unattended nevertheless make their marks. Several authors have

explained in detail the differences between the two sides of the brain.[28] The left brain is the seat of analytic understanding, and lexical activity. Heightened states of sensitivity encourage new connections of information bits, often in great arrays. This type of perception/information processing, linear and sequential, is mastered by computers. Conversely, the right brain is the seat of holistic understanding and imagery. Heightened states of sensitivity encourage deep awareness and understanding in terms of broad concepts. This type of perception/information processing, parallel and instantaneous, can never be duplicated by computers.

"The chief characteristic of the mind is to be constantly describing itself."[29]

What we perceive may be just a reflection of our instruments of perception. "The emergent awareness of one's own spontaneous inner activity produces a feedback effect, which can generate a new pattern of action, affect or fantasy."[30] Design is something everyone is doing all the time because it is "the constant attempt to understand an everchanging, highly complex existence by imposing order in it."[31] What you want to be is what you see and what you get. The psychologist Piaget formalized adaptive mechanisms of accomodation and assimilation in his study of children. He describes accomodation as our response to external stimuli and the progressive extension of understanding.

Assimilation, on the other hand, is the effect of these stimuli on the ongoing cognitive system, the relation of the parts to the whole of consciousness. Piaget explains further: "It is because the objects perceived by the child are thus assimilated to the act of grasping-that is to say, because they have set in motion the need to grasp and allow it to be gratified-that the hand reaches for them, and not because an association has been established between a visual image and the reflex of prehension (grasping)." "It is this active relationship between subject and the objects that are charged with meaning which creates the association"(between visual stimulus and motor response)"and not the association which creates this relationship."[32] In other words, baby gets the idea because baby plays the game.

For Piaget, our adaptation and assimilation to the environment, "presupposes schemata;" we have a dream. "We must believe in the potential associations we seek,"[33] one aspect of the theories of self-actualizing. We can make our dreams come true.[34] The ability to carry out one's plan is enhanced if one can imagine oneself executing the necessary actions. Wyler has studied increased emphasis on self-constructs in social learning and cognitive style theories. Lewin (1935) called it "means-end cognizance". Bandura (1977) called it "expectations of self-efficacy".

"Modern theory of change makes it possible to indentify cycles of external change and internal organizing response that create a process and that continuosly modify it. The nature of the process derives from cumulative response and analysis of it explains the evolution of the process."[35] Tavis goes on to expand our understanding of what a process is in terms of parts, factors, and types. Parts include transforming activity, states, material flow, contextual flow, energy, signals and sources. Factors include the technical core or the principal activities of the process, the environment, and boundary spanning activities. Types include long-linked (single flow), mediating (single flow) and intensive (multi flow). Processes repeated in view of collective expectations create a system. Tavis then describes the management of process change as the essence of organizing. That is the way an office is, works and grows. "Planning produces structure based on understanding key variables, such as purpose of the organization and support for individual performance."[36]

"Tasks of any substance take time development and elaboration...the structure of tasks over time are at war with the clean desk syndrome..."[37]

"Dreams and the life of the mind, which accompany all human activities, should be nurtured by habitat..."[38]

PROCESS:
Work Is Fantasy

"Realization is the merging of thought and feeling at the closest rapport of the mind and the psyche, the source of what the thing wants to be."[39]

"Without fantasy there is no life, no love, no culture. Life's romantic travels must be lost in mysterious wanderings, something must be left to chance."[40]

Victorian culture emphasized creative imagination and fantasy activities as a basic element of daily life. Most upper class or nouveau riche homes were "elaborate environments in which to act out personal dreams."[41] The homes of the middle class were not far behind, with a fantasy of wealth in the explosion of architectural gingerbread, and every other overwrought object evocative and ostentatious. It was indeed a very rich mixture.

Nevertheless, it remains true even today that one usually must dream or play at doing something before possibly trying it for real. "Daydreaming reflects attempts to explore the future."[42] From flying a plane to riding a bike, from being President to being a father, it is always effective. In a Rolling Stone interview Joseph Heller, author of Catch-22, said "Yes, I'm not sure young people can be satisfied with success. I think people who want to write would agree with that. For me, the satisfaction was in wanting to be a writer, in trying to be a writer, in writing and in submitting what I did. Even though I wasn't published until I was 22, I began submitting stories when I was about 10 or 11. But the satisfaction came in that there were connections between me and certain wants and needs - needs of the imagination, of the emotions to express fantasies, and it was private, and yet could become public. I know I wanted to be a famous writer when I was 10, but the want was its own satisfaction. I felt I would be a famous writer, but the feeling was its own daydream.

Just having that daydream was a very important reward." [43]

Richard "Jaws" Dreyfuss said, "I'm just trying to deal with the world as it presents itself to me today, which is only lately becoming half as much fun as dealing with the whole thing as a fantasy."[44] Having a fantasy and achieving it are two very different things. "The uneducated are often frustrated by the inability to perceive the steps to achievement of fantasies...compared to middle class youth, whose life is structured from early age in terms of a series of linked subgoals..."[45] The metaphors of the mind are the world it perceives.

"The plains, caves, caverns of my memory, with its manifold and spacious chambers, wonderfully furnished with innumerable stores."[46]

Brooke Astor has recommended the following in her comment on the wisdom of follies: "...build a little folly of your own - not so pretentious, perhaps, but a little eight-by-eight foot retreat where you can read or write or contemplate a favorite picture or treasured object...it can be an extension of oneself...or created simply to delight the senses..."[47]

PROCESS:
Work Is Memory

Memory function is dependent on initial storage of impressions and sense data in the process of assimilation. In other words, to see or understand something means to "already remember it", at least in the short term. The psychologist Singer explains "effective interpretation of incoming stimuli requires a matching process between a visual or auditory image (event outside the brain) and a centrally emitted image (event inside the brain). The new stimuli create reverberatory activity in short tern memory." Tomkins studies how memory is a process of informational compression or reduction, involving images and symbols, the language of the brain. Since the process is rapid (but not instantaneous), it is a good idea when giving instructions or important information to speak slowly or repeat the message. Often the inability to remember something is due to failure of initial information storage. Sometimes a sudden external event, (like a ringing telephone), or a rapid shift of internal cognitive material (As a sudden remembering that you have a date for lunch), can block an event or idea, from memory storage. Or else sometimes the impression is just too vague or fleeting to stick.[48]

In order to retain memory of whatever is stored, and keep it in active file, it must be used or reviewed periodically. The reason why most of us can't remember half of the stuff we learn is because we don't use it. Singer explains that "even stored material must be revived into consciousness and rehearsed for its continued storage."[49] Diaries, see-at-glance calendars, books and brochures piled on the desk, and all of the other accessories of office work in progress fuction as memory cues to help us continue juggling the thousand and one ideas, goals, projects and plans that compete for channel space in the brain.

Memory can play tricks on us, like deja vu. We have all had the strange feeling on occasion that we have been there before, or the nagging impression that we're sure we know somebody or something, but it slipped the mind. Many studies have been done to correlate memory ability to various factors of personality such as motility. People who can sit still and listen generally score higher in memory, visual imagery and basic creativity tests.[50]

In the "invisible mansion" of the mind, it is very difficult to be in two rooms at the same time, however quickly we pass through them. Singer found that "nonrecall was not related to dream content, but to non-integrational compatibility of sleep and waking states."[51] "The antagonism between motor activity and dream recall brings to mind Proust's words that he could recapture former being 'dehors de l'action, de la jouissance immediate' and that in such a moment he did not dare budge lest he lose the refound memory of the past."[52]

Recall can be a relative and active venture with fantasy and vice versa.[53] This interdependence is illustrated by the possibility "to sense a fantastic dimension in almost anything since our perceptions are all relative and based on our dynamic state of being."[54] Both perceptions and being can be influenced and stimulated by the environment. "Memory and fantasy are active participants in every environmental experience, and are often the essence...yet the pleasure of environmental reminiscence is infrequent...in consious recall, we seek the emotion once associated with place," such as recalling the melodramatic intensity of college life as well as the old halls around the quad.[55]

Memories of vacation, as well as of childhood are a strong popular and personal element of the habitat. Memories of places associated with happy times form the basis of many environmental preferences in adults. One problem with the office may be the impression of it as opposite of such preferred places as the inglenook by the fireplace, or the backyard treehouse. "Active fantasy was often an essential part of even that first structuring of close emotional ties to place."[56] "Research suggests...that subjective experience is more related to distant memories, fleeting images, irrelevant imaginings and fanciful anticipations...than to rational processes."[57]

PROCESS:
Work Is Daydream

We can see, through the commonly understood activities of memory and fantasy, the ways daydreams influence our relationships with so-called real world. Actually, daydreaming is an integral element of the spontaneous mental activity in the ongoing stream of consciousness,"that ever-changing constellation of memories, sense data, fantasies, rational thoughts and images that constitute our moment to moment awareness." Even solving complex mathematical problems involves techniques of mental imagery and concept sorting/matching which are first developed in the play of normal daydream process. The powers of the human imagination grow in the exercise of daydreams.[58]

One of the most obvious functions of daydreaming, especially at work, is to cope with or escape from a dull environment. "The daydream competes for attention with other events. It is generally a weaker stimulus and can emerge chiefly under conditions in which external stimuli are greatly reduced...daydreaming and thinking are highly valued and personl activities and are likely to emerge as soon as external demands are even moderately reduced."[59] Night dreams represent the "ongoing reverberatory activity of the brain under conditions where external stimulation is reduced."(Ulman 1958). Even when the work task/environment provides stimulation, the capacity for daydreaming is enormous (Antrobus Singer 1964). The variety of both internal and external environments permit and sustain higher levels of energy, allowing higher productivity over the long term in spite of increased frequency of mental coffee breaks, which used to be called wool gathering.

In some cases, daydreaming ability can be carried to the extreme. "A skilled daydreamer can carry on an elaborate fantasy while dogs bark, children scream, whistles blow and lights flash."[60] We've all had the experience of being so lost in thought that we don't hear the telephone ring, or arrive at our destination without remembering the road travelled. At the opposite end of the spectrum, some people can place an absolute priority on attention to external events as a defense against self-awareness. This so-called "flight into reality" seems characteristic of managers and analysts who are mesmerized by the superficial data regarding operational performance, and who cannot seem to understand group functions in simple human terms.

The task/environment encounters daydream phenomenon in two ways. Through perceptual variety, the task/environment may directly stimulate imagery and associational thoughts. Through perceptual monotony, the task/environment may indirectly drive people to create internal activity and interest. However, this is much easier for some people than for others. For example, in one study by Singer, "children who indicated a greater degree of daydreaming also provided more internal entertainment or stimulation for themselves during the waiting period, (during which they also showed greater motor restraint correlated to greater imagination by Rorschach M responses as studied by Riess), while children who showed less disposition to daydream were also the ones who made more direct perceptual responses and seemed to depend more heavily on what Piaget has called

'the stimulus nutriment'

of the environment."[61] It seems that common sense is right again.

Task/environments lacking in variety can create frustration and anxiety in all but highly imaginative people. Oddly, it seems that so called imaginative/creative people may actually have a higher tolerance for dull environments than less sensitive individuals. Could this ability to discover more in less be one of the reasons that architects and designers have pursued a minimal aesthetic for so many years? Formal psychology has begun the investigations behind such conjecture. Hebb's work in 1949 and 1959 initiated the "deeper look — both at the ongoing reverberatory activity of brain process and at the motivating properties of the environment in its complexity and unfamiliarity."[62] Others, such as Tomkins have studied the relation of mental affect/emotion to the "density of neural stimulation provided by the complexity or novelty of environmental stimuli." As Singer points out, such a cognitive approach avoids the problems of drive reduction theory and behaviorism.

Therefore, those who create or provide environments should consider whether they desire people to be affected in one of the following four ways:

- stimulated and entertained through environmental variety, as in a theater;

- confused and distracted through variety overload, as on the commercial strip;

- repressed and frustrated through environmental monotony, as in a prison;

- stimulated and entertained from within through lack of distraction, as is a room for meditation.

The basic choice is whether the most appropriate mode of work is exuberant, disciplined or some combination of the two. "The daydream is one manifestation of an ability to attend to internally produced stimuli or to use those stimuli to construct a new stimulus source less monotonous or less threatening than some external stimulus patterns."[63] "In whatever the uses to which daydreaming may be put, however, it seems best regarded as a capacity available to most persons for assigning priorities to particular sets of spontaneous internally produced cognitive stimuli."[64]

Though everyone is unique as an individual, many people share some basic daydream behavior patterns. Some groups of people have a greater need or proclivity for daydreaming. "Analysis of questionaire studies shows that daydreaming is a remarkably widespread common occurrence when people are alone and in restful motor states. It is a human function that chiefly involves resort to visual imagery and is strongly oriented towards future interpersonal behavior."[65] Common topics of daydreams include personal concerns, sexual satisfaction, altruistic concern, and unusual good fortune. Factors which have been shown in experiments to affect daydreaming frequency and content include: age, education, socio-economic status, rural/urban background, family constellation and ethnic cultural background.[66]

The results show that high frequency daydreamers as a group usually include the young, maternal identifiers, urban and rural inhabitants (ie. non-suburbanites) and the upwardly mobile. High frequency dreamers have more fantastic and unlikely images, less anxious and more heroic. They seem to achieve in their dreams "a dimension of experience along which any number of possible human behaviors can be played out with relative impunity."[67] Though intelligence does not seem to affect daydreaming frequency, consistent results have linked creativity and imagination to daydreaming activity.

Surprisingly, "it may be that despite common reference to the private world of the psychotic, the hospitalized schizophrenic may show less frequent and more impoverished daydreaming than the normal," the man on the street.[68] Obsessional personality types, for example, the introverts and the workaholic perfectionists, show a higher frequency of fantasy activity than hysterical personality types such as the extroverts or the hotheaded loud-mouths. In fact most studies seem to indicate that daydreaming and fantasy are basic tools used to control emotions and nervous physical behavior, effects which are necessary to allow creative activities to blossom.

Different modes of daydreaming operate at different times for different purposes. One basic type is the repeated self-consistent, elaborate fantasies, such as "when I get my promotion" or "when my ship comes in". The other basic type is the general free pattern of reverie, with its stream of associations and interior monologue as well as the occasional elaborated fantasies of a spontaneous nature associated with particular problems or chains of thought – the "what if..." sequences.

Our day to day use of mental imagery can be both preventive and constructive:

- adaptive escapism — in response to dull environments, periods of waiting or falling asleep;

- self-regulation — in order to control emotions an impulsive activity;

- self-awareness — personal attitudes and biases may be revealed in the patterns of dreams and daydreams;

- trance — for the pleasure of meditation, contemplation or self-absorbed rapture, like getting lost in the deep reading experience or watching the rain;
- creativity and aesthetics — the products of daydreams bring great pleasure to both the artist and the audience.

Singer specifies five principle patterns of daydreaming besides general one outlined above:
- objective controlled thoughtfulness (mental chess);
- poorly controlled kaleidoscopic daydreams (colors and patterns);
- self-recriminating daydreaming ("if only I had done");
- neurotic self-conscious daydreaming ("if I don't do this");
- autistic daydreaming ("he's out cold").

These patterns may each exhibit personalized wish fulfillment, fleeting planful imagery, novel constructions and symbolic transformations.

It seems that the primary dimensions of daydreaming and general mental activity are:
- simple—complex;
- reminiscent—planful, theoretical;
- personal—impersonal.[69]

To review, the three mental modalities are:
- lexical-analytic (left brain);
- imagery, holistic (right brain);
- enactive (cortical motor areas/libric system).[70]

Unfortunately, non-rational creative thinking has been termed regressive relative to rational thought, or as a primary operation versus a secondary one, "The fact that we conceptualize the mind of Beethoven...of Bergman...as representing a somehow more primitive style of thought than a mathematician...or lawyer... perhaps reflects more the weakness of our theories than the weakness of imagery, fantasy and creative imagination." "It is important not to view the enactive and image systems as early developemental forms that must be superseded by the verbal or lexical system, but rather that all three systems, in their complex interrelationships are of equal importance."[71]

PROCESS:
Work Is Creativity

By this time the reader may realize that the concepts of this discussion are overlapping and interdependent. We seem to be moving back and forth across the same ground, each time in a slightly different direction. That is how the web of understanding is woven.

"Mothers in our society tend to represent inhibition of impulses and also to foster aesthetic interest while fathers represent action tendencies and the external environment."[72] "Strong imaginations would seem a likely source for original thought and cognitive variety...perhaps persons with strong ideational tendency are slower to respond (in creative problem solving) because internal stimuli generated by the problem require synthesizing, hence postponing problem resolution and delaying external display."[73]

The creative process is an ongoing evolution of attitude that shapes one's relationship to self and environment. The female principle with which religious art is deeply involved is associated with sensitivity, and linked traditionally to a passive or receptive relationship with the world, as a prerequisite of creativity. Sensitivity is nurtured by observing the worlds without and within. The female principle and creativity are also linked to the dark, mysterious, unpredictable side of the self. Creativity is something fresh that arises out of the absence of preconceived ideas or socialized reality. Intuition is ideas springing from untapped parts of the self.

52 TRANSFORMING YOUR OFFICE

Worlds can be created by the human imagination. Our society does not encourage the creative use of fantasy in most types of activity outside the circle of the arts. When one lets go of preconceptions, when one looks at things upside down, or inside out, an infinite range of new possibilities is revealed. Fantasy and daydreaming stir the stew of sense data, impressions and ideas within us, sending to the bubbling surface just the juicy chunks needed to serve the current project.

Such fortuitous events usually occur after a period of concentration and immersion in a project and subsequent incubation of the ingredients. The solutions seem to deliver themselves automatically when we are in a relaxed, daydreaming state, such as on the bus, in the bath or in bed. Other fruitful times include floating, sunbathing, sailing, or exhaustion, fasting and sleep deprivation. Some of these are of course more enjoyable than others. It all depends on how high you prefer your rate of neural fire.

Voluntary social withdrawal into fantasy is a natural cycle for periods of synthesis and integration.[74] "Dr. Einstein did not sit in the middle of Grand Central Station in order best to study...he went into seclusion..."[75]

Great insights come when least expected- are they:

- Messages from the right side of the brain to the left?
- Internal probabilities of neural structure?
- Endorphins or other biochemicals linked to emotional triggers of pleasure and pain?
- Compensation for neurosis anxieties?
- Cosmic radiation evidenced in mental mutations?
- Astral force fields?
- Brain waves of the collective unconscious?
- Words of the All-Mighty?
- Some people need an answer, others don't.

Another scenario of the creative process for the office:

- make a salad of data resources;
- set aside all preconceptions and initial responses;
- begin environmental/information background/interference patterns;
- review data and daydream;
- voila — the concept arrives on a silver platter!

"If you organize your ignorance, tackling the situations as an overall project, probing all aspects at the same time, you find unexpected aperatures, vistas, breakthroughs..."[76] "Start all problem solving with universal categories."[77] Don't force it, but don't let the balloon touch the ground either.

The reader should recall the points discussed earlier in this chapter regarding the "original question" and the way in which ideas are born out of the chance combination of events, fostered by environment.

"The semantical debate on the interrelation of rational and irrational mental functions", is endless controversy and "confirms, the necessity and validity of the irrational modes of thought."[78] "We always find at the origin of invention an irrational element on which the spirit of submission has no hold, and which escapes all constraint."[79] Andre Gide expressed the idea that classical works are beautiful only by virtue of their subjugated romanticism.

Creative imagination: the faculty that helps us to pass from the level of conception to the level of realization...in the course of my labors I suddenly stumble upon something unexpected. At the proper time I put it to profitable use. The gift of chance is a collaboration which is imminently bound up with the inertia of the creative process and is heavy with possibilities which are unsolicited and come most appositley to temper the inevitable over-rigorousness of the naked will."[80]

"All creation presupposes at its origin a sort of appetite that is brought on by the foretaste of discovery. This foretaste of the creative act (anticipation) accompanies the intuitive grasp of an unknown entity already possessed; but not yet intelligible..."[81]

— PROCESS 55

A classic example of the creative work process, as pursued by Leonardo da Vinci is described below in the words of Sir Kenneth Clark, creator of the book and television series, **Civilization**:[82] "The most important collection (of Leonardo's famous notebooks) is the great **scrapbook** of notes and drawings in the Ambrosian Library, known as the **Codice Atlantico**. It contains about four thousand sheets of various dates and sizes dealing with every subject, all covered with Leonardo's minute writing..." "In order to increase and display his mastery of architecture, engineering (the conduct of masques and pageants as required duties of the official artificier of Sforza), he began to keep notes of machinery and ingeneous devices of all sorts, either seen or invented." He followed the example of a treatise by Francesco di Giorgio. The notebooks were begun when Leonardo was about 30. They are literally a record of the stream of his consciousness, including both observations and reflections.

"But almost from the first, Leonardo's penetrating grasp of construction, combined with his restless curiosity, gave his notes on technical matters a more general value. He was not content to record how a thing worked: he wished to find out why. It is this curiosity which transformed a technician into a scientist. We can watch the process at work in the manuscripts. First there are questions about the construction of certain machines, then, under the influence of Archimedes, questions about the first principles of dynamics. Finally, questions which had never been asked before about winds, clouds, the age of the earth, generation, the human heart. Mere curiosity has become profound scientific research, independent of the technical interest which had preceded it...(the notebooks) are full of reminders to borrow or consult books, and research has shown how many passages which used to be taken as original discoveries are copied word for word from other authors..."

Leonardo mistrusted generalities and preferred to dwell on the details and specific information content of perceptual reality. "Leonardo's lack of synthetic faculty, perceptible in the notebooks as a whole, is partly responsible for their complete lack of order."

The point here is that imagination and art must be stimulated and fed. One cannot create in a vacuum. We need ideas, materials, energy and so on. The reuse and juxtaposition of myths, dreams, symbols and styles is a large part of the design treasure chest which many people are reluctant to consider, for a variety of reasons.

Another point is the need for a rigorous method to generate the mechanisms of creativity. Art is act. "...an entity...will not take shape, except by the action of a constantly vigilant technique...it is the idea of discovery and hardwork that attracts me...the very act of putting my work on paper, of, as we say,

kneading the dough,

is for me inseparable from the pleasure of creation..."[83]

"A philosopher...is a sort of intellectual yokel who gapes and stares at what sensible people take for granted, a person who cannot get rid of the feeling that the barest facts of everyday life are unbelievably odd."[84]

PROCESS:
Work Is Ritual

"The Dionysian elements which set the imagination of the artist in motion and make the life sap rise must be properly subjugated before they intoxicate us and must finally be made to submit to the law: Apollo demands it."[85]

"There is one art, no more no less, To do all things with artlessness."[86]

To many people, the word "ritual" conjures up the image of exotic religious procedures; but ritual has a much broader meaning. Almost any activity can be considered a ritual, from raising a flag to tying a tie, from making a pot of coffee to compiling the annual report. The difference between a ritual and a routine is the care with which it is executed. In ancient times, when men did everything for the pleasure of their gods, rather than their managers or clients, they followed an exact, prescribed course of actions. Things had to be done the correct way each and every time. The high level of concentration in any ritual procedure creates a unique spirit of basic awareness and openess. Ritual activities have tremendous variety, but this unique spirit is specific, singular and natural.

Ritual behavior can signify or communicate to others the importance of the elements involved or the task at hand. General rituals include ceremonies, meditation, fervent prayer, encounter with art, solitude, retreat, silence, trance, poetry, oratory, continuous singing, chanting, spinning, jumping, dancing, aerobic exercise, any sport, making war, making love, encounter with others, encounter with nature, flower arranging, farming and gardening, domestic arts, crafts, fine arts, etc., as well as any possible function of office work.

Hopi farmers don't grow beans, they relate to beans which releases the beaness within each seed and thus food comes into being.

Karma yoga is the use of ordinary experience as a path of awakening. Cosmic dreams can visit us when we contemplate stone to touch our origins. Hunters from prehistoric times used the religious magic of cave paintings and dance to capture the spirit of their prey. Sioux warriors walk "in-a-sacred manner."

In every ritual, there is a natural balance and interdependence of place and process, which is developed through rehearsal, practice makes perfect. Repetition is the nature of ritual. Whatever is repeated is appreciated in new ways. This is the concept of discipline. Refinement of operation is a virtue which brings its own rewards of personal satisfaction; but can also bring other benefits of raises, promotions, higher productivity, better client relations and general business growth."...the life of pleasure cannot be maintained without a certain asceticism, as in the time and effort for a woman to keep her hair and face in fine condition, for the weaving of exquisite textiles, or for the preparation of superior food."[87]

"I am first to recognize that daring is the motive force of the finest and greatest acts, which is all the more reason for not putting it unthinkingly at the service of disorder and base cravings in a desire to cause sensation at any price. I approve of daring. I set no limits to it. But likewise, there are no limits to the mischief wrought by arbitrary acts."[88]

The quarrying and cutting of stone was once a religious activity with reverence for the natural law, as understood in the medieval attitude of piety and humility. Stone is noble material because it is extracted from the depths of the earth. Man takes on the role of time when he extracts materials yielded more slowly by natural process. There was a time when the ritual of the activity acknowledged such presumption, rather than taking it for granted. With cultural progress and enlightenment, the emphasis shifted from the emotional to the intellectual spheres. During the rediscovery of the ancient Mediterranean world by 18th century Europeans, curious stone objects and artifacts became the most prized collectibles. Anything made of stone seems to carry a special ritual significance.[89]

Rituals tend to make us more sensitive to our surroundings. They can precipitate a direct sensory, emotional, intellectual and spiritual encounter with the overwhelming facts of existence; of being alive, and of one's place in the evolution of life and the cosmos. Carl Sagan has renewed this primary ritual element in the act of star gazing.[90]

The peak experience can occur through any creative or ritual process. It is the high moment of insight which highlights our lives and often changes our understanding of reality or the task at hand. Peak experience is characterized by spontaneous awareness of: ego transcendence, self-trust, ends rather than means, time/space disorientation, receptivity, transcendence of dichotomies (or opposites), strong self-identity, and, surprisingly, either a strong sense of free will or of humility and surrender. In memory, past peaks are references to make future peaks more easily accessible.[91] Research into the bio-chemical aspects of peak experience is revealing startling evidence of how the body can literally turn itself on.

Direct sensory involvement with our environment can bring not only pleasure, but also development of inner awareness. "The faculty of creating goes hand in hand with the gift of observation."[92] "In the realm of the creative, the great introspectionists have excelled because they were capable of describing with clarity a great variety of sensory experiences."[93] People who are less dogmatic at the ideational level are more discriminating in sensory levels (Kaplan and Singer 1963). "Rich experiences are more to be desired than property and bank accounts...a style of life will be colorful and elegant...an adventure."[94]

PROCESS:
Work Is Play

"The mother, a regular and requent companion, created an atmosphere novel, yet not startling, hence arousing the positive affect of interest...the playful exploration and creativity in the nuturing of her child, which is one of the greatest arts of 'femininity'..."and of mentoring in general. [95]

The office can provide an atmosphere "novel, yet not startling" which might encourage the developement of sensitivity in its inhabitants over time. But more importantly, stimulating office environments can also foster good morale on a daily basis. Relaxation and a feeling of being at play seem to promote a deeper, more productive involvement with office work, as opposed to wild abandoned craziness which would not be appropriate under any but the most extreme circumstances.

At the very least, a mildly playful atmosphere in the office seems to allow and encourage the individual to put more energy into his assigned tasks than he otherwise might. But first, the office person needs to understand how to turn work into play. For most people work means something someone else wants you to do, while play means something that you want to do. Surprisingly, it is not difficult to bring them together in any office activity.

We first experience play as children. Swinging on the swings, riding a bike or digging in the dirt, were pursued for only the personal feelings of interest and pleasure. Little did we realize, even then work and play were blended. We may think we played because we wanted to. But our parents wanted us to play because it was an important way for us to grow and learn.

Play is the child's work. "The parent, then, in permitting free play and free exploration, establishes a basic atmosphere in which the child can maximize his affective experiences of interest and joy through a series of detailed discriminations...the stuff of a richly sensitive inner experience..."[96]

The child's play actvities are usually spontaneous and constantly changing in response to external and internal environments. Such a process can be very useful in the office because it keeps a person in touch with current and meaningful events or goals instead of getting buried under mountains of directives and data.

Openness and looseness may be more appropriate to office work which involves generating creative ideas, as in the case of the marketing executive who flips through magazines, watches television or walks around bouncing ideas off the walls with his associates. But openness and looseness might also help clerical and secretarial personnel from getting so wrapped up in an assignment given yesterday that they don't notice the memo on the desk saying that everything has changed, (again), and that a new task must be given top priority. Psychologists have noted that children under tremendous drive pressure are less likely to explore or play. Acceptance of work as play might help people from getting frustrated or angry every time the goals/rules of a project/game are changed. Less anger means more energy to get on with the job.

As mentioned earlier, well-developed skills of mental play can help a person to create or understand new concepts and relationships more quickly and easily. "Thomkins' has provided the beginnings of a theory of memory, which may suggest how fantasy play material can become stored as a series of images or conversations available more or less on demand without overt reconstruction."[97] Inventiveness, which is first practiced for personal pleasure alone, can develop into inventiveness which also serves the goals of the team or organization. Keeping a sense of play at the office can prevent work efforts from getting bogged down or losing momentum. Maintaining forward motion, following the bouncing ball, and keeping the game alive are basic methods for achieving success or at least survival, especially in the face of uncertainties. .

Game theories have been applied to office life on many different levels, from the individual to organizations as a whole. Without repeating all the various discussions of this concept, here, they can be summarized around the issues of motivations and strategies. The analogy of games is an easy way to communicate specific goals and the methods for achieving them, since most people understand the nature of games from their childhood experience. Here the focus must be on the basics of "what is the job?" and "how are we going to do it?" Detailed analysis of all interrelated phenomena is not necessary and might even become a distraction from the central purpose for both the individual person and the collective office.

When office games revolve around power politics they can become counterproductive. Unfortunately, many people feel it is necessary to put much of their time and effort into playing power games for their own survival or advancement. Because of this, the primary activities of the office can suffer, or even become totally neglected. It is too bad that many office organizations continually reward such behaviour. The squeaky wheels always seem to get greased first.

However, there are other secondary office games which might enhance productivity instead of detracting from it. The positive, playful nature of nostalgia, ceremony or perhaps even voyeurism can make the office routine more immediately enjoyable for the individual, as well as reinforcing the sense of a common, shared purpose. Such a secondary game might take the form of an office that is physically set up like a toy town.

Office life can often be improved by a person relating to his job on the level of a private fantasy, or game which does not degenerate into power play. In the face of extremely negative circumstances, Studs Terkel has noted that in order to maintain a Without repeating all the various discussions of this concept . occasional games to keep up their spirits and energies.[98] Another reason for treating office work as play can be the simple basic desire of each person to be acknowledged as a distinct individual. We don't have to be hailed as something tremendously special, but it can be a great achievement in some offices for a person to rise above anonymity and be called by name.

Injecting office behavior with elements of play is one way to make a personal mark on the routine and be remembered for it. Such play can be inspired by childhood games from hopscotch to hot potato. Or it might take a cue from myths, legends, and fantasies of popular movies, classic books, or television programs. The incorporation of fantasy play can be as entertaining for one's neighbors as for oneself. This might make for good times at the office, without interfering in productive activities. Telling jokes can be as useful as strong leadership or fast typing.

It's tough to have a sense of play in the office if a person feels so constantly on the defensive that he must construct all kinds of physical and operational barriers between himself and everyone else. Just like in the animal world, there is a big difference between living in a protective shell like a clam and soaring the skies like a bird who sacrifices a no-risk existence in favor of freedom and pleasure in action. Play is the freedom of feeling and doing which must enter into the very fabric of being itself, if a person wishes to lead a fulfilling life and career. That doesn't mean a person can get along without being upset from time to time, or escape from all worries and cares. It just means that person must make sure the genuine concerns don't take over and make him a prisoner inside himself.

Many philosophers and poets have expressed this wonderfully basic idea: that success without a full life is no success at all, but only an empty delusion. An honestly open recognition of "the inevitable coexistence of good and bad constitutes a freedom which creates both joy and anxiety,"[99] according to the anthropologist Klee. Yet anxiety is not necessarily a negative thing, if it reflects the individual's "willingness to tolerate his fears openly and directly."[100] The idea of an open office is meaningless if the individuals in it cannot first be open with themselves.

TWO
POWER

POWER:
People

"...you can't eat for eight hours a day, nor drink for eight hours a day, nor make love for eight hours a day — all you can do for eight hours is work, which is the reason why man makes himself and everybody else so miserable and unhappy..."[1]

"Business is business, people are people, nothing is perfect, but anything could be better."[2]

"too many people talking at me, I can't hear a word they're saying..."[3]

"Those who know do not talk. Those who talk do not know."[4]

If information is the essence of the office, then the way that information is created and transmitted deserves the highest priority of attention. From the personal to the global scale, this needs to be an on-going activity for everyone. The biggest problem is that most people assume the intended message was received intact. We often consider it embarrassing to ask for a verification to the question, "Do you know what I mean?" Unless we hear the message repeated back verbatim, we can't be sure it was indeed received. This type of closure in communication becomes increasingly necessary at a time when it also seems increasingly rare. Overlooking the receiver's personal and unique perspective on our thoughts or observations is like throwing food away - it's a waste. Of course even in a medium sized organization this can consume a great deal of time. Some offices handle the situation efficiently with announcement boards, free-flowing memo traffic, or even an age-old suggestion box. But the dialogue is usually stifled by anxiety and paranoia in the face of peer competition and the general hierarchy of power. People share their thoughts and energies effectively only when they feel they are doing so in a common interest.

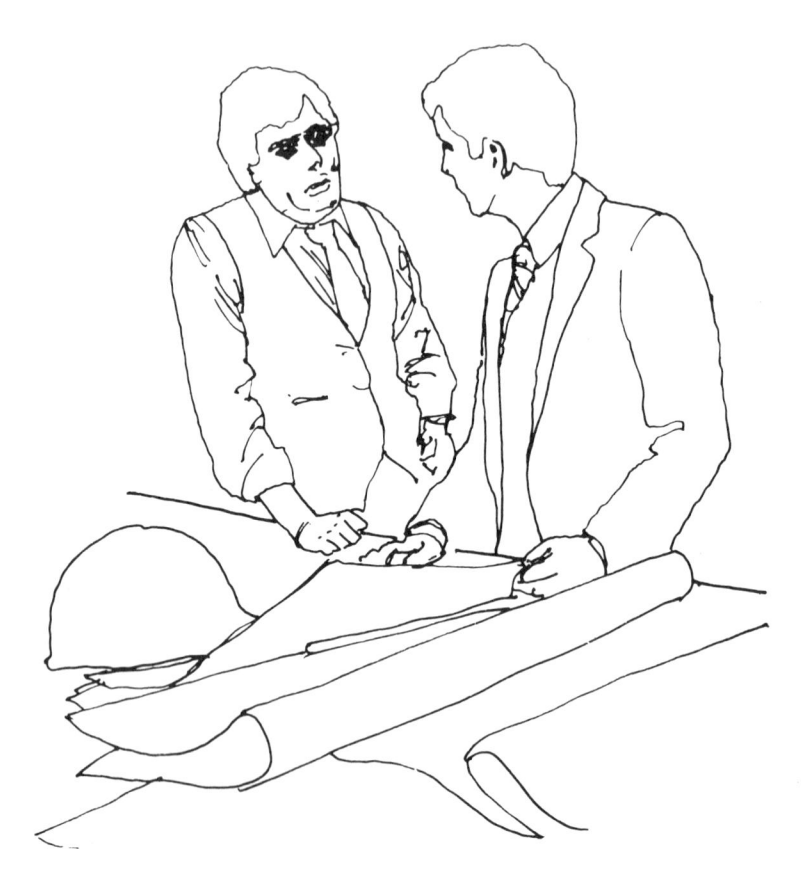

"One thinks of Piaget's charming description of the egocentric speech of nursery school children, side by side, who verbalize at length about their individual games without, however, really attempting to communicate."[5]

Most people feel very attached to their ideas and are offended by even the slightest criticism. The situation doesn't appear likely to improve until people can achieve a more detached attitude and have a sense of themselves independent of the products or ideas which they handle. We need to feel that the units of communication are like a hot potato, to be tossed along, rather than something precious to cling to. That is why there are so many footnotes in this book. People worry unnecessarily about being original when it is easy make new combinations of ideas from almost any point in the information flow.

We are generally not aware of the ways in which our habits of communication reflect their origins in animal behaviors. Messages of aggression, courtship or alarm may be explicit or implicit elements of our communication with each other. Every aspect of human behavior can be involved in the exchange of information. The smiling response between the parent and child is the basis for development of communication.[6]

The relative position and angle of speaker to listener in the office expresses degrees of friendliness and informality.[7] The most comfortable and natural is the 90 degree angle, especially for lounge and table seating. This is much more relaxed than the formal face-to-face, yet not quite as familiar as the side-by-side. The arrangement of furniture in waiting areas should be clustered to promote conversation groups, except in certain types of medical practices, where the seating should give each individual a sense of privacy or at least elbow room.

The arrangement of furniture in the private office should respond to the type of communcation carried out there. Flexible arrangements are highly desirable, as is enough surplus of positions that the vistors are confronted with a choice, which decision can set the tone of the exchange.

In table seating the lesson of the round table is still valid — but the power focus at a table head can also be necessary and effective. Therefore, a good choice in a conference table would be a broad or narrow oval, depending on which end of the spectrum is more desirable, or on the shape of the room. Usually conference rooms are shaped to fit the table, and not the other way around.

Another variable of conversational position is the vertical dimension; for the following choices there is an infinite range of effects depending on whether all participants are the same position or not: all of the variations of sitting, such as with good posture, slouched, feet on the desk, sitting on the desk, closed or open leg cross, ankle cross, leaning forward, leaning backward, sitting on the floor, kneeling, squatting, lying down, standing, one foot on a chair, standing on a soap box, leaning against a wall with the body or the hand, standing on the head or the hands, sitting on the hands, sitting with the head in the hands, and on and on. Most of the time we sense the meaning behind the choices subconsciously, but when the implications of body positions can vary as much from culture to culture as language, the international executive should be careful of his assumptions.

In almost every office, the conference room is a special place, where pomp and circumstance survives and communications can become true rituals.

Postures of conversation are connected by movement and articulated with gesture. "The process of moving in and out of space is a communications act triggering secondary contacts."[8] Our movements can be as natural as we wish, subtle or dramatic and so on. Most of all, movement can be a source of pleasure for both the self and others. Richness of human exchange derives from the incorporation of movement, from the singer on the stage to the executive presentation.

The typical office environment treats movement as something to be avoided. The negative medical effects of sitting down all day are a familiar litany of sore backs, weak hearts and hemorrhoids. Very few offices have special exercise rooms for employees, and typical working hours might allow only the top executives to make it to a health club and back during lunch time. In pleasant weather one can go for a walk outside, provided that there is a place to go besides the parking lot. In addition to the benefit of physical and psychological refreshment which can greatly enhance productivity following a period of exercise, one can also make good use of the time to incubate ideas for the issues, problems or tasks of the day. This can happen at any time of movement in the office, especially on trips to the washroom or on coffee breaks. Sometimes it seems that more useful ideas are discovered or communicated during these moments of relaxation than during the regular hum of the day.

Since it is not likely that offices will institute formal calisthenic periods or group singing of the company song, perhaps there are other ways to integrate physical refreshment into office life. One way of forcing people to shake their legs a few times a day may be by placing the restrooms and coffee machines in a remote rather than central location. Or perhaps one could put a radio on the Xerox machine to generate masking sound, and then encourage people to dance while they are making copies. Another way of improving circulation is to have alternate work stations for standing versus sitting.

Boaz, the father of cultural anthropology, asserted that the motor habits of expressive cultures can be very revealing. Psychologists have begun to study the many implications of this condition and its relation to other aspects of human behavior. For example, Witken's studies in 1962 showed that differences in perceptual orientation may develop which represent important differences in human personality."

Returning to the subject of office communication, we mentioned previously the role of gestures to enhance verbal and visual exchange. There is an endless variety of meaningful ways to use the hands and arms in concert with the rest of the body. The French have a way of puffing out the cheeks and raising the eyebrows to indicate a form of surprise or interest. Anxiety or impatience is universally communicated by tapping the foot or drumming the fingers on a table. The litany of facial expressions used in the office is endless. Many of the movements and gestures, as well as verbal expressions found in any particular office are part of a private sub-culture derived from the observation and imitation of the senior personnel. More often than not, this type of humor is focused on those who are respected, or at least well known for their unique personalities.

One example of the imitating gesture assimilated into a group culture is the phenomenon of the Cambridge Philosophical Hand Movements, which began as exaggerated imitations of the famous philosopher Wittgenstein when he was a lecturer there. The sophisticated use of hand signals at the stock exchange is a fascinating example of an almost primitive ritual preserved and patched into a computerized tele-communications network of instant world-wide information. The instantaneous nature of hand signals is the reason for their perpetuation.

Most of us work in more relaxed surroundings than the stock exchange. Common rules of etiquette still apply in the general office. A cardinal rule of good manners is to treat others always with kindness and respect. A review of etiquette manuals, such as the classic by Amy Vanderbilt,[10] updated recently by Letitia Bladridge, suggests the many ways this can be done. Being friendly and natural are good basic points of etiquette. A smile, a shake of the hands, a bow, or a salam should bracket any personal encounter, no matter what the nature of the exchange. A curt nod of the head or a wave of the hand is not really appropriate in any non-feudal society.

Paying attention to someone when they are speaking to you is not only etiquette, but good business too. Maintaining eye contact and controlling fidgeting all help concentration. Unless you know someone will keep talking until you interrupt them, it is a good idea not to interrupt until they're through. If they speak very slowly and you're not sure if they have finished, it's easy to ask, "May I make a comment here?", without sounding silly or disrespectful.

Currently, one of the more ticklish situations is precipitated by the spreading use of microcassette tape-recorders, which are used not only for dictation, but also for recording telephone conversations and meetings in lieu of taking notes or as a precautionary back-up. Usually, if the other party understands that you want to use the tape recorder so that you can concentrate more directly on what they're saying, they won't object. It would not be surprising if executives begin adding a safety clause to the end of each such tape, qualifying its impact on existing contractual relations in order to prevent future legal hassles. Such an "off the record" clause may preserve the candidness so vital in direct personal business communications.

The other peculiar problem of etiquette in the office exists between men and women who are peers, friends and associates. The practice of greeting such a friend with a kiss on the cheek may seem perfectly natural out on the street, but some people take it the wrong way in the office. Other fine points of office manners include knowing how to drop names, and knowing what to say when the boss walks up to you at the water cooler.

One of the biggest and most variable aspects of office etiquette is the dress code. There are still some employers who consider anything less than a coat and tie to be improper office attire. Such requirements do not limit the expression of personal indentity. The cut, fabric and color of the clothes offer a wide range of possible choices reflecting social status, level of education, cultural sophistication, wealth, or imagination. Unusual accessories such as tie tacs and pins can create a touch of whimsy and character that brings the whole look together. Even the Secretary of Commerce knows when to wear his cowboy boots. Style is power. Sources for inspiration can be found in fashion magazines, window shopping or just walking the city streets to see what the Beautiful People are wearing.

Clothes are also a great way to have fun. They can be used for emotional support, such as, dressing up in special ways to counter negative moods of depression, anger and frustration. Clothes can signal the passage of time and the change of seasons. They set the tone or style of daily exchange. Within limits, people behave in response to what they and others wear. Clothes can bring direct sensual pleasure to the wearer and the audience. Colors delight the eyes and textures please the touch, besides keeping us warm or cool, as necessary. The movement of fabrics can enhance the movements of the body. We are all part of the daily show.

The only way to develop good taste in clothes is to build a wardrobe — slowly. One can begin with classic styles in natural fabrics, such as wool, cotton or silk, if you can afford the time and expense to take care of them. A core of interchangeable separates may be used as a versatile travel wardrobe. There should be at least one very good and one moderate quality suit for both the warm and cold season, regardless of the local climate. It is a good idea not to wear the same clothes all the time, in order to preserve the fabric as well as minimize the boredom of associates. Like Linus, many people seem to carry their security blankets for years in the form of a favorite sweater or jacket. Good shoes and a good raincoat are essential. Special items may be added as the budget permits; perhaps a few good things each season. Fashion can be fickle from year to year, so one should either beware of the fads or play them with caution. Since trends of new clothes are closely associated with the currently popular revival fashions, collecting a few antique accent pieces from the 20's, 30's, 40's, 50's and even the 60's can vitalize a closet. Clothing from parents and grandparents are a handy resource.

Other points of grooming and hygiene are as absolutely essential as they are taken for granted. Well-cut, clean brushed hair, and clean manicured hands (if you don't have to work with artists materials) are a general requirement of civilized office life. Men of course, should be clean shaven, or have well-trimmed beards or mustaches. Complexion and tooth care are as important for good health as for making a good impression.

"...you're only pretty as you feel..."[11]

Of course the most important part of the wardrobe is the body itself. Getting into shape and perfecting total body conditioning should be a constant project for everyone, not just the Olympic athletes. Though we've heard it all before, the tired adages are worth repeating: quit smoking, cut down on drinking, try not to eat so much junk food, etc. These things will increase sensitivity and enjoyment of all sorts of gastronomic and culinary pleasures.

And if you are too fond of meat to give it up for moral reasons, perhaps the rising costs may reduce its role in your diet. A good cut of meat is enjoyable from time to time, but cooking with vegetables can be much more interesting. Its up to you to design your self and your life.

Who you are and what you are is up to you too, within certain limits. Goals for personal development and role models initiate with the figures of our parents: either we want to be like them or the opposite of them. Usually it is some combination of the two. Additional attributes are picked up from reading or the movies or real life encounters, and layered onto the model.

Many goals for personal development stem from the envy of schoolmates or associates or neighbors.[12] As discussed in the first chapter, daydreaming plays an important function in our testing of future behavior. Sometimes the roles are never intended to be realized, and are instead an elaboration of the life we lead. However, if we intend to reach the goals in reality, we must follow a progression of stages for acting out the chosen roles. Such a series might be as follows. Think about examples seen of other people or fictional characters in the role. Imagine doing it and then try it for run with a friend, in a mirror, or on a bartender. But at some point we just have to cinch our belt, and dive in to do it for real. We don't have to worry about being perfect since nobody is; just as long as we don't take ourselves too seriously.

"Feeling and dream have no measure, they have no language, and everyone's dream is singular..."[13]

And then there must always be some time to act crazy. You have to get it out of your system. Many tribal myths and rituals offer serious orientation to behavior rarely encouraged in daily life: shamanistic insanity, glossolalia, Halloween and the office Christmas party.

POWER:
The Individual

"The landscape of the human innerworld of landmarks, coordinates, hierarchies and especially boundaries, serves, we believe, as the only humane starting point for the organization of space around us..."[14]

Everyone lives in a bubble of personal space whose boundaries seem to expand and contract to meet the changing situations. On top of a mountain or in the middle of the prairie, the boundaries can expand to the horizon. Riding on a crowded bus they can be contracted to the skin. But the boundary is always there. The territory which we occupy in the office must have clearly defined boundaries if we are to feel comfortable and productive.

But a boundary doesn't necessarily have to be a stone wall. Dominion over space can be demonstrated by its use and personalization. If I put pictures on the wall, the wall becomes mine. If I put my books on the table the table becomes mine. In order to really be in a place, we have to become involved with it and make it part of ourselves. A person needs a little more than a place to hang a hat. When a space is shared by a group of people, they usually end up personalizing areas of it as a natural extension of themselves, like an umbilical cord linking them emotionally with the place.

"The architectural boundary exists to encourage and ritualize activities which are sacred to the family (or the individual), and its destruction or exaggeration can sap the vitality of both the family and the public domain in which it resides."[15]

The way a boundary is created may become the act of personalizing the place, full height floor to ceiling walls, or movable partition systems are not the only way. Colored poles can mark out points along the boundary as well as a canopy hanging overhead, or an area rug on the floor. The manner in which the boundaries of a place are defined, and the way its interior becomes layered with personal artifacts mixed in with elements of work, is an expression of the image and individuality of the occupant, whether he consciously participated in this process of habitation or not. At the most advanced level, the personalization of a place can become one of the most effective tools for acting out and achieving one's goals, by projecting the image we most want others to receive, as well as by reinforcing our faith in our own abilities. In this way, the place we occupy in the office is not only a refuge but a source of power.

These basic functions of the individual's place in the office have been confused over the years with territorial status games and retreat from the demands of continuous social interaction. Buckminster Fuller has noted that "a minimum regenerative territory is a basic ecological requirement of all living species."[16] For the office animal, this is understood most commonly as a private office, the attainment of which has come to be one of the highest goals in the business jungle. The chain of command need not always display itself as an overt pecking order. The strain of interpersonal conflict can bring out the desire for privacy as a defensive reaction, rather than a positive move to improve efficiency or productivity. "The most profound complaint, aside from non-recognition and the nature of the job is being spied on".[17] Freud developed the idea that for most people, work at least gives a secure place in a portion of reality in the human community. "Is it any wonder that in such surreal circumstances (as exist in many offices) that...

status rather than work itself becomes important."[18]

"In defence of privacy as a status statement, many seniors are deprived of key exposure to office activity."[19] In cases where the activities of senior personnel are highly interrelated, the private office may be a spatial dysfunction separating people who would be more effective if they worked closer together.

This is one of the main reasons for the open system, which is often justified only on the basis of economy and flexibility. The primary dissatisfactions with open office systems come from their inability to convey status with the same power as the old enclosed office. Another problem with the open system is the proliferation of noise, distracting movements of people, and the inability to "shut the door".

Of course, all of these problems can be resolved with careful planning, the proper equipment and some education for the users. Being within ear shot of those whose actions directly affect yours and vice versa can save a great deal of time, and catch problems in the early stages of developement. But when the need for privacy is actually a need for confidentiality, as in the meetings of clients and lawyers, a private office may still be necessary. If conference facilities can be shared or alternated, then group or team offices may be a more productive arrangement, provided of course that the people can get along with each other. It is much more desireable to spend the days in the company of friends, and stimulating, supportive colleagues, than isolated in a private office. "Overconcern for privacy may indicate retreat from responsibility and sagging motivation..."[20]

In fact, the creative personnel in design offices almost always use this kind of shared arrangement with great success. Unfortunately, the administrative officers seem a little slow to catch on. They seem unable to function when they cannot stretch their arms in front of a few panes of glass and say "This is mine", rather than sharing a more spectacular view with the group. Executive personnel shouldn't necessaily be mixed in with the staff, but at least they can interact with each other a little more, departmental structures permitting. If the need for privacy is actually a need for secrecy or camouflaging the maneuvers of corporate intrigue, then this opportunity for a better office is lost.

"As status orientation is converted to goal orientation, the use of space and hierarchical furnishings will undergo major readjustment...the great diversity in what one may be required to do in an office does not allow a continuation of sterile uniformity with status as the only definition."[21]

Another question regarding the individual in the office is the issue of neatness. Apparent neatness is a function of both the tools of the individual's work process, as well as his personal effects. Most offices are far too sterile, impersonal and boring. What is done in order to present an illusion of a well-coordinated operation, can often inhibit a truly effective operation. On the other hand, some people seem to work in the middle of a pig pen, which would seem to prohibit any sort of orderly process entirely. Of course, there is a middle road, which does not stifle all forms of work or personal display, but instead organizes areas or regions within the individual work space as well as within the overall organization in which these functions may occur. People may be instructed and encouraged to use them in such a way that they become adapted to the needs of the individual, so that useful and stimulating variety arises within the organizing structure. This is Probst's concept of the Action Office. "Tasks of any substance take time, development elaboration...the structure of tasks over time are at war with the clean desk syndrome."[22]

Those who provide the office habitat should consider these needs of the individual carefully, if they wish to have as Lord Mountbatten said to the crew of the HMS Kelly, "a happy and efficient ship..."

POWER:
The Team

"...I get by with a little help from my friends..."[23]
Any office larger than one person cannot function without effective teamwork. Some offices use teams more than others, or at least more overtly. In a team the tasks are ultimately broken down and assigned to individuals. The earlier that this happens, the greater the intensity of participation by all team members, and the less likely for someone to feel left out or behind or that what they are doing is not an important contribution. No matter what the level of skill, intelligence, or experience required for any particular task of the team, all tasks are of equal importance if they are necessary to complete the job. The executive with a good secretary knows how fortunate he is, and realizes that he is probably twice as productive than he otherwise might be without her help.

The ability to assist each other is the most important aspect of teamwork. That doesn't mean to do the other guy's work for him, but don't throw obstacles in his path either. Any information which we stumble on should automatically be passed on to those who might be able to use it, either now or in the future. The inability for people to work together is the biggest factor in bad attitudes towards office work. "The exminister of the labour market in Sweden pointed out in his opening speech at a conference on "psychological stress factors in the working environment" that a third of those who report sick usually plead fatigue, stress and nervous indisposition as causes of absenteeism."[24]

The control of team turf seems to be more a preoccupation with feudal games than with future business goals. This tendency is reinforced whenever the appearance of power is treated as the substance of power. Once this habit is broken, the games will cease. The control of turf as a means for control of information, and vice versa, is slightlty more complex. In most cases, the location and relation of individual work stations is primarily meant as the symbolic representation of the various relationships within the team, and thus representative of other factors of the individual's position and attitude: structure, organization, stress, working hours, promotion, salaries, job content, etc.

There are two basic ways to think about teams. One is intradepartmental, or within the department, cutting across the levels of hierarchy. The other is interdepartmental, or between departments, but is usually confined to a specific level of the hierarchy. These two basic types of teams may be used separately or simultaneously to execute all sorts of standard and special office functions. A team coordinator does not necessarily make any more decisions than the other team members, but he functions to insure that everyone is aware of what everyone else is doing, if they can't do this for themselves, and also provides the linkage between the team and other groups. Because of this, the cooridinator may have extra power.

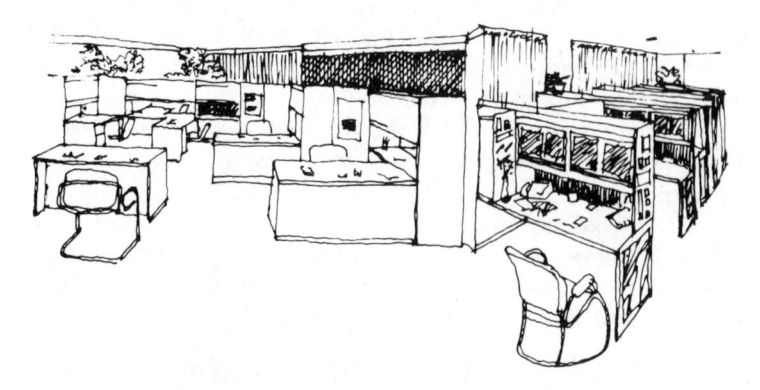

All of this talk about helping and sharing and being together does not imply that no one should be in charge. That would be foolishness. There can't be all chiefs and no Indians, because somebody has to do the work. When decisions are made collectively, the group needs a figure head, or spokesman to relate to other groups. This is an ancient habit of human relations. Nevertheless, authority needs to be handled with skill and tact. We all can't be like General Patton. The office is not the army, unless of course it really is the army. Even there the difference between brow-beating, inspiring and guiding a staff are recognized.

When a team coordinator is also responsible for team performance, he becomes a manager. In academic circles there are three basic approaches to management, known as Theory X, Theory Y, and most recently Theory Z. Theory X assumes that most people avoid resonsibility and that the role of management is to set objectives and exercise control. Theory Y assumes that most people seek responsibility and that the role of management is to provide the challenge and encouragement necessary for top performance. Theory Z, which is founded in the traditional habits of Japanese culture, a small crowded place where people were forced to learn to cooperate with each other centuries ago, emphasizes mutuality, long range planning and consensus decision-making.

In Theory Z, senior personel are trained to be creative problem solvers by serving in all departments of the operation on a rotation basis. Though this causes a much slower developement of specific skills, it does produce a cadre of non-specialist, analysts who are well aware of how the relations between the different groups and interests in the firm operate.[25] Traditionally in America, the specialized career paths in business, such as marketing, finance, management, produce much higher levels of professional skills in the earlier years.

No country or theory can claim a patent on the basic concepts of teamwork. Individual skills and knowledge of interelationships are both equally necessary for team success. What is very different from one culture to the next is the style and tradition of team play. It is claimed that due to increasingly "competitive" world circumstances, "U.S. companies may have no choice but to nurture a Japanese style spirit of corporate teamwork."

What about the Yankee style of teamwork?

Energy and enthusiasm are as necessary as ever. It is a deep misunderstanding around the world to think that the Yankee fighting spirit is based any less on commitment to community than it is on so called rugged-individualism. The Yankee style is part and parcel of the myths and legends of our national heritage. But it is also a style which must evolve and change if it is to remain a vital resource of power.

No matter what the style of the team, a clear definition of groups goals and individual roles is absolutely necessary to avoid confusion and redundancy. These may change from day to day in response to the juggernaut of the project, but that is fine as long as everyone is kept abreast of the evolution. Once a goal has been set, every effort must be made to complete it in a thorough and professional manner, within the budget. A good exercise is post-project review that openly and honestly judges the degree of task closure by the team. This should not be connected with salary or individual performance reviews, or to the annual report. It is often true that we need narrative fantasies with which to interpret the universe or to amuse ourselves, but that must be differentiated from those who "are allowed to assume a performance fantasy, never following up on many actions they endorse or initiate, who exhibit a continuing failure of intentions, however well-meaning." Judgements should be circumspect, since anyone can bite off more than he/she can chew from time to time, and most projects end up being twice as complex as originally imagined. That is what the office is for — to work things out which cannot be totally planned in advance.

Style, image and function of team operations cannot be separated anymore than what you do from how you do it. The way in which a task is performed should be appropriate to the task and the setting, just as the setting should be appropriate to the task and the style of its execution. Contributing an image may or may not be an essential part of the direct job, or it may be the entire content of the job. In an age of increasing image-consciousness, we are all well aware of how an image can affect not only the functions of the office, but also the collective expectations of those functions too. People can function in their contribution to the team of image, as in Victorian times when women were decorative accessories, symbolic of cultural sophistication.[26] Images can communicate values and generate energy. Images are power.

POWER:
The Organization

The power of an organization is rooted in the fact that once it is initiated it seems to have a life and a mind of its own, regardless of the wishes of its participants and creators. This is because the flow of energy, information and activities has immediate, dynamic and long-term effects on each other which are of infinite variety and possibility. Controlling a large organization can be something like trying to drive a hurricane. The basic forms of organizations seem to have some predictable tendencies which may be related to possible directions for growth and change.

The power of the organization is its members and their relation to each other and to their context of action. As a metaphorical example, I suggest the permanent earth sculpture by Walter de Maria, **The Lightning Field**, located in New Mexico: a huge open expanse of uninhabited rough grassland surrounded by distant mountains under the violently changeable sky. In the middle of this space, in an area one mile by one kilometer square, stand 400 narrow stainless steel poles, spaced 220 feet apart in rectangular array. The poles' sharp tips define a level plane about 20 feet above ground, which generates a most magnificent display of natural electromagnetic discharge.[27] That is organization. It is also a work of art.

The tangible and intangible aspects of an organization are reflections of each other. Just as the parts are related to the whole, so all interdependent factors must compliment each other on every level of form and meaning. The form of an organization is often illustrated by an organization chart, which usually shows only the most formal distribution of power and responsibility. Other charts may illustrate the flows of information, or the informal structures of teams and project groups. The story of the organization is the sum of all of these. It is like looking at the same flower through different types of lenses.

Though most formal organization charts are some variation on the classic pyramid concept, other angles of perception may reveal all sorts of forms. The wide variety of possible forms can suggest new ideas for organizational operation. Either way you look at it, it is still a question of design. The following discussion of organizational form is a paraphrase of Ching's chapter on spatial organization, which makes an interesting application to the organization of people.[28]

Centralized organizations...

are stable compositions in which rings, or layers of secondary units are grouped around the primary influential element. This unifying element is generally regular in form and also of a critical mass large enough to draw the secondary elements about it. If the secondary elements are relatively equivalent with each other, their arrangement around the central element may be in response to external conditions. A centrallized form is basically non-directional, or static. The possible patterns of flow within it may be radial, loops or spirals, usually terminating in the central unit. An example or metaphor of centralized organization is a daisy.

Linear organizations...

are composed of units linked in series. The units may be directly connected with each other or they may be connected by means of a common spine. Whether the units are indentical, or different, they share the condition of exposure to external conditions. Elements of special importance can be located in the middle or at the ends of the series, or they may be located at pivotal points where the series changes direction. This kind of articulation produces a segmented form. Because of their characteristic length, linear organizations entail a significant amount of internal movement. They also signify endless growth possibilities. The series can be left dangling, terminated in a dominant element, or merged into external conditions. Linear organizations are inherently the most flexible. They may be used as a barrier between two different fields or as an enclosing element. Very large or special elements can be connected to a linear organization in a second order phenomenon. The loop is a linear organization fed back into itself.

Radial organizations...

combine aspects of both centralized and linear organizations. They consist of a dominant central element from which a number of linear organizations extend in a radial manner. Whereas a centralized organization is by nature inwardly focused, a radial organization reaches out to the external conditions. These extensions may be developed with any of the options for the linear forms. They may be handled in a similar way, one to the next, to maintain the regularity of the whole, or they may be different in order to respond to special requirements. The most dynamic radial form is the pinwheel. A spider's web is another example of radial organization.

Clustered organizations...

depend on the proximity of the elements to each other. Because the pattern does not originate from a specific geometrical concept, the form of a clustered organization is flexible and can accept growth and change easily without affecting basic character. The clustering can involve the nearness of the elements: they may touch, or overlap, or simply be arranged with some sort of enclosing element or condition. A linear or feature element may be introduced to focus the clustering, which remains less compact, dense or regular than the truely geometric forms. Since there is no inherent place of power within the pattern of a clustered organization, the significance of an element may be revealed by its relative size or orientation to the overall pattern. Symmetry or an axial condition can modify the looseness of the clustering and foster the relative expression of significance between the elements. Clustered organizations are often described as being relatively organic or humanistic as opposed to the geometric organizations.

Grid organizations...

are defined by a regular pattern of points and lines which are extended into multiple dimensions. The principal shape may be a rectangular array, or some other regular geometric pattern such as the hexagonal honeycomb, or intricate crystal. The organizing power of a grid results from the regularity and continuity of its pattern that pervades the elements it organizes. The pattern of reference points and lines create repetitive modules within which the elements of the organization can be located. This reference system then provides the linkages between the elements beyond those of simple proximity, or those created independently and in contrast to the grid itself. Formal manipulations allow the grid to grow and change as it extends its inherent structure into the field of external conditions. These manipulations include shifting reference points to generate internal irregularities, which create potentially hierarchical relationships, interrupt the pattern entirely, or dislocate some section of it in relation to the whole. This is what happens when one TV show spins off from another. Finally, the grid can transform its character internally by shifting the emphasis from the reference points and lines to the elements in the array.

The planning of the organization "produces a structure based on the understanding of key variables, such as the purpose of the organization and support mechanisms required for individual and team performance."[29] An organization is the process of organizing.[30] The first level of understanding is the system, which is defined simply as the grouping of parts that operate together for a common purpose.[31] A system is a process if it effects material closure through a fulfillment of the collective expectations. Process must involve repeated operations, which are usually based on the reduction and then the restoration of universality in the material flow, like taking money out of the bank, multiplying it and then putting it back' in.

"Change is the master, grace is the mistress."[32]

The goal of every organization is to provide a general performance base with adjustable facilities for user self-adaptation.[33] Adaptability is critical because there are no crystal balls to help perfect everything in advance. The program or description of an organization or operation must be updated on a regular basis. The leverages of organizational behavior are part of the management technique, and benefit from the continuous feedback and guidance of an in-house primary planner who is not swept away in the daily flow of crisis. The actions which focus on alleviating a stress point in the organizational process are the responses to conditions by which the organization accomodates and assimilates its environment. That is how the organization grows.[34] Other angles of modern organizational theory besides social psychology include goal orientation, communications and cybernetics, systems and interdependency. In other words, organizing is the management of process change and not just process execution.[35]

When, where and how an organization changes can be determined in many ways — from the top down, the bottom up, the inside out, the outside in, and so on. Each case is applicable under certain conditions. A common situation in an organization occurs when a staff member executing an operation encounters specific conditions which lead him to realize an alternate improved method. It is the responsibility of the staff member to judge whether he must seek formal approvals for his idea, or whether to proceed with it as an experimental test, keeping everything on a more informal and immediate level. That is the pressure of being a staff member. If formal approval seems necessary, one shouldn't be afraid to seek it. Similar to asking for the keys to the car, it is wise to pick a time when the authority in charge is in good spirits and not too busy, and when one happens to be in good graces with the powers that be, or perhaps after one has recently achieved some distinction.

One of the biggest problems in managing organizational operation and change is the tendency noted by Weick for groups to evaluate solutions before all of the possibilities have been assembled. The lack of thoroughness and circumspection in the typical shot-gun approach is often falsely justified in the name of efficiency or urgency. "We just can't spend any more time on this", unfortunately often leads to even greater wastes on down the road. In fact, Weick explains, groups often look for solutions even before they are certain what the problem is.

Leaving this abstact level for a moment, we can touch on one of the most basic problems of organizational behavior — the problem of being on time, flextime not withstanding. For junior personnel it should be almost a religious habit, In fact, it's a good idea to come early and have some time for coffee or casual gossip: time to wake up and get into the groove so that when the seniors roll in you're already cranking away. Besides being impressed, they may catch a little of your energy and spirit. Also, it is a good idea if the boss is not always the last one to arrive.

In reference to quitting time, it may be necessary to stay late occasionally, but overtime can become exaggerated beyond the call of duty, a dis-service to the organization, and the signal of a need for change in operations. Too much overtime can be mentally debilitating and counterproductive. Time spent relaxing with family and friends, or enjoying recreation and entertainment is just as important for success and well-being as reading the right magazines, if not more so.

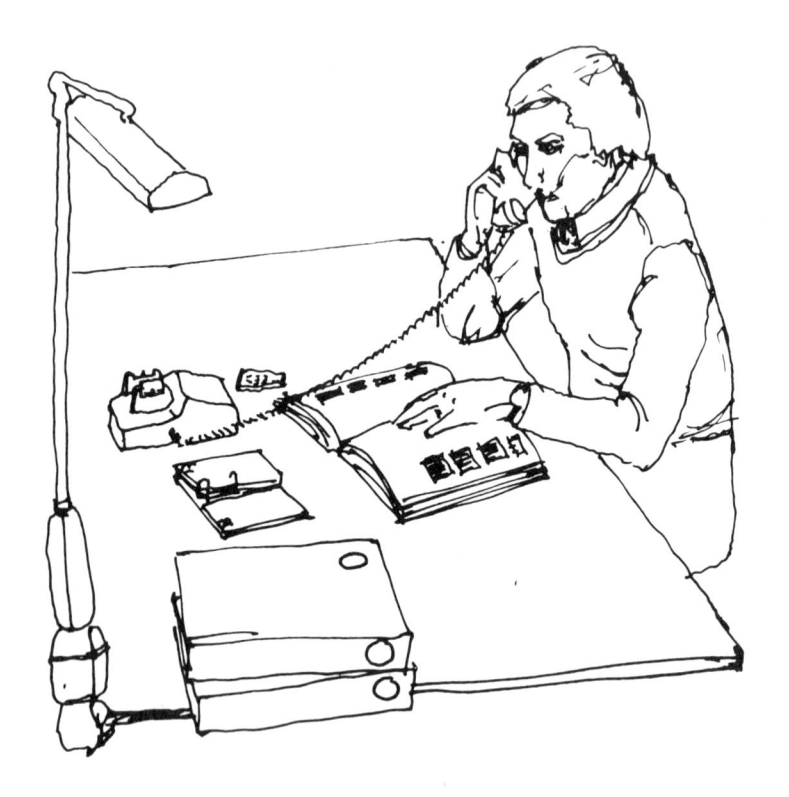

POWER:
Information

"The flood of information creates an overload situation in which the unusable obscures the critical."[36]

This is a universal fact of life of which we are all aware. The accelerating rate of change in the world doesn't help the situation. Trying to keep up with the constant flow of news and events which can affect any office operation almost seems a hopeless task. News and business magazines, journals and newspapers, along with daily and weekly television reports provide an invaluable service in condensing and focusing the facts for general use. But these vehicles of information can also monopolize a person's time, or cause him to forget about other important sources of useful facts and ideas, such as reading books which may require extra effort. Industry forums, conferences and trade shows are another vital source of information. The most difficult sources to manage are those delivered by serendipity, such as the chance encounter with a person, a book casually flipped through, or an unanticipated television show, can deliver surprises of tremendous practical utility for life in the office.

The focus of planning on communications involves three basic networks: general information, instructions and opinions.[37] These may be stored according to how the data was generated, or how it will be used or both. As an office may be divided into line and staff groups, so the information may be divided between generic versus project files, or by the department or services to which it is usually related. The method of information storage should allow for many possible interdependent connections between sets of data. The actual systems of storage can suggest or generate new combinations of facts and ideas automatically. That is their power.

The traditional mode of information storage in the office is words and images printed on paper. The paper is usually kept in manilla folders which in turn fill up the miles of filing cabinet drawers. This bulky, unwieldy system began giving ground to the electronic revolution through the use of microfilm and microfiche systems, which store information in tiny images on transparent film. But this system is also rather inflexible when compared to the electronic storage of information through computers and word processors. As the preferred memory unit, punch cards and magnetic tapes are being outpaced by the floppy disk, which looks like a soft RPM record, but which can hold up to 200,000 bits of information. Other types of disks, tapes and cartridges offer many opportunities for a much more useful, accessible office information base.

By reducing the space requirements of old-fashioned filing

cabinets, these new electronic systems give the space back to the people. The infinite potential for systems expansion in connection with input and output terminals through telephone lines, cable networks or via satellite, along with 2-D and 3-D visualization and voice-activation options, promises a fantastic future for the world of information.

An important part of information storage is the program for recycling data for review and analysis of the organizations track record, and as a basis for future planning. Most difficult of all is the task of keeping information under control. "Purging of files must be programmed and defined."[38] For the most part, files are purged and synthesized as they are used, and assimilated through experience. Still, it is necessary for some formal definitions concerning what information should be kept active indefinitely, and how long to keep the rest active, and what the nature of the dead files should be. Tax and contractual laws, as well as common sense dictate retaining data for some time after it is no longer current. The reality of the situation can vary tremendously from one office to the next. Obviously, law offices seem to require the greatest amount of file space per key person than any other operation.

For any type of office, the most difficult information to handle is that which is generated in a very personal way. Notes from meetings and telephone calls, or telex messages may relate to many different files or categories of information storage. Sometimes it is quite difficult to decide just where to file things, and duplication or cross-referencing can make the whole storage system very unmanageable.

In whatever manner information is stored, it should be done in a way that can grow and change along with the organization. Antiquated filing and communication systems can cripple even the most hard-charging teams. "...rows of enclosure connected by corridors fits an organizational behavior format already rare; linear communications in a totally vertical organization..."[39]

Fortuitous, unplanned encounters of data as an aid to information processing and transformation in the course of office operations has already been mentioned several times. Most offices are woefully conservative and counter-productive in their approach to the display of information in use. Charts, maps, outlines, bulletin boards, blackboards, participatory group log books handled as wall size posters, or inprocess filing systems of envelopes tacked on a wall are a few of the possible formal and informal methods to achieve useful information display. In general, the most neglected opportunity for display is the vertical dimension from the use of stacking file trays to the walls themselves.

"Suppression of relevant visual display is a serious deficiency in present office culture,...display is efficient if kept current, it can explain work, define individuality, and relieve memory..."[40]

In the battle against the flood of information, human is often in partnership with machine. The relation is best handled when each party is fully aware of both his strengths and weaknesses, which in this case are very complimentary. As Buckminster Fuller has explained, "The human brain stored questions plus all the individual's heritage of chromosomes — administered subconsciously operative experience responses, represent, in progressive sum total,

the uniquely variant integral known as the individual man...

Computers cannot in millions of years generate enough unexpected interferences to occasion enough original questions to be further integrated to approximate even an average individual, let alone each of a trillion individuals' lives and their half a septillion interrelationships and the unpredictable interferences thereby generated...", (while on the other hand)... "it's very clear that the computer is already making man obsolete as a differentiato, that is, as a specialist...the entrepreneur of the future must be half designer, half scientist and all generalist..."[41]

POWER:
Servants

"...all really inhabited space bears the essence of the notion of home..."[42]

In the home it is taken for granted that the refrigerator, the sofa, the television, the bed, along with everything else is there to serve the residents. Somewhere along the line, the roles were reversed at the office. The secretary works for her typewriter, the clerk for his computer, the executive for his telephone. The machine dictates the life of the office inhabitant, instead of the other way around. Everyone has labored under these conditions for so long that they almost seem unavoidable. Only recently has sophisticated technology permitted the tailoring of the office equipment to the detailed personal requirements of individuals and organizations. A vast array of interlocking components proliferates into infinite numbers of possible combinations. Now is the critical moment of office evolution at which point human beings must once again gain the upper hand.

The first line of battle should be the subjugation of office furniture, those legions of insidiously conceived objects which totally dominate the character and operation of the office today, and are most generally at odds with the true needs of those human beings who see no other choice than to work at a desk. "Desk job" has meant office work since the turn of the century, evidence of a gross misconception and arbitrary limitation that has been passed along unchallenged for generations. Since the early 1960s, more flexible forms of work stations have appeared. This is the beginning of a liberation from the tyranny of "a real office is a desk/credenza/chair" syndrome. Other elements at the office which should be servants of the inhabitants, rather than dictators of abstract efficiency principles, are the basic environmental conditions of light, air, sound and space.

As stated several times already, the essence of the office is information. Nearly every piece of primary office equipment is related to information processing. Everything was done by word of mouth or hand until the beginning of the Renaissance, when mechanical printing was invented. This marvelous discovery was not brought into general office use until the invention of the typewriter in 1868. Shortly thereafter, the second most common piece of office equipment, the telephone, was invented in 1876 by Alexander Graham Bell. Prior to that information which required rapid transmission was sent by telegraph. However, in those days the cables were an outside collective service. The telephone and the typewriter brought the sophisticated information processing apparatus to the individual's fingertips. Another critical component of information processing in the office is the computer. For centuries, the ancient Chinese abacus remained the most advanced device for calculations, until the advent of the slide rule.

A quantum leap occured in 1946 with the invention of the first electronic computer, ENIAC. Some believe the sophistication of computers is the next major step in human evolution because of their tremendous expansion of the brain's natural analytic capacities. Made possible with the invention of silicon chip circuitry, the miniaturization of computers and their appearance as pocket calculators has certainly revolutionized our lives. Other significant information-related devices include: the camera, radio, television,and sound recording and reproduction equipment. In fact, every form or process of the media industries is useful and available to any office operation.

Each year brings forth some new developement, such as the refinement of existing equipment, or the combination of different devices or processes for a very unique effect. The classic example of this is the developement of the photo copier. Once a luxury item, now almost every office has at least one at its disposal, either in-house or just around the corner at a quickie printer. Originally, copies of typewritten materials were restricted to the use of carbon paper, a messy and primitive technique that was very inflexible and difficult to change or correct. One usually had to start over. An intermediate machine in the evolution was the mimeograph, whose distinctive smell and shiny paper brings back memories for many of us. When true xerography of positive originals emerged in 1938, the explosion of information jumped another level.

Flexible correction and duplication processes have come together only recently in the word processor. In the past, the abyss of the "circular file" received a continuous stream of torn and wadded pieces of paper, projects abandoned at the first stumble. Then a miracle happened with the discovery of the eraser, which was married to the pencil in 1858. The ink eraser and typewriter eraser followed soon after. Complaints of dust and wasted time led to correction tapes, which are held against the original covering the error with a pasty substance smashed into the paper by the typewriter key. Liquid corrction fluids had the extra advantage of coming in assorted colors to match any stationary and were also useful for correcting hand-written copy. Continued complaints concerning waste of time and lightheadedness from blowing on the liquids led to the novel approach of correction tapes that actually lift the offending ink right off the paper, instead of covering it.

The concepts of duplication and flexibility came together with the mating of typewriter keyboard, computer, and high speed printers, and video display in the modern word processing package. This revolutionary integration of several information processes into a highly productive and flexible unit is the first step to the so-called paperless office. Word processing, computer, CRT and printout units can be connected to each other or to a "mother machine", called a mainframe or central processing unit with a gargantuan memory. Virtually eliminating the major snags in the production of printed material, the new equipment still needs refinements and coordination with other modes of information operation.

Though computer graphics have come a long way, its printed line drawings or dot matrices are still light years away from the complexity and subtlety of hand produced graphics. In combination with video display and image processors, the new artistic achievements have eclipsed the great masters; a fact we have all enjoyed in the special effects of science fiction films, or even the "title page" graphics bracketing of video programs. When these magical tools can be incorporated through computers and video discs with printers and display terminals so that both

verbal and visual
information can be processed together, the real baroque period of information evolution will have arrived.

As long as the doodles and abstract scribbles unconsciously created during a meeting can be a key to understanding new concepts and information, they must be saved and stored. We mentioned earlier the use of micro-cassettes to record meetings and telephone calls. When the devices of automatic transcription are developed to put the "meeting" into the cassette files, perhaps they can be accompanied by the "meeting response" picked up on a magnetically sensitive doodle pad that is scanned by the central recorder processors and put in the files "verbatim", i.e. exactly as drawn. The current state of light pens and other graph plotters must be raised from the level of chiseled cuneiform to the brushwork of calligraphy.

Other flights of fancy include voice-activated 3-dimensional images or holograms for use by designers, especially in the preliminary exploration or brain-storming phases of their work, which are currently stifled and slowed by the inflexibility of hand drawing each option and variation on slips of yellow tracing paper aptly called "trash".

Until the various machines for information and image processing can virtually blend in with the whirlpools of the human stream of consciousness, our most vital creative endeavors may remain imprisoned in such unbelievably archaic methods. The continuing evolution of office information equipment promises the liberation of human beings from a tremendous amount of drudgery. If we are not careful and honest with ourselves about the tasks we want to accomplish, we may all end up working for the machines instead of them working for us. Our information processing equipment must serve with the same inspiring focus of data and flexibility as Leonardo's notebooks. The full potential of all the sophisticated office information machines cannot be realized until people believe they will make life easier, and that cannot happen until the terminals are flexible and portable and as easy to use as pocket calculators.

Since such far reaching developements will take some time to accomplish, the office today must still accomodate information on paper. The principle agent of this accomodation is the traditional filing cabinet.

Vertical files have drawers which are wide enough to accomodate a single file of letter or legal size, and files fill the drawer from front to back. Lateral files, which were developed more recently, have drawers which are deep enough to accomodate single files and files fill the drawer from side to side. Lateral files have several advantages over vertical files, even though they have slightly less capacity drawer for drawer. The top provides an extra work surface, which is especially useful when sorting things before filing, or when searching the files to find a particular item or document. Also, lateral file drawers protrude only 18 inches into the space, instead of 30 inches for vertical files, thus causing less disturbance of circulation patterns.

Another advantage of lateral files is that they generally have a more classy, contemporary appearance than vertical files. Both types come in 2-drawer, 3-drawer and 4-drawer sizes. Five drawer vertical files can be found second-hand, but they are no longer manufactured. Lateral files also come in various standard widths: 24, 30, 36, 42 inches. In order to use the full height of space along a wall, up to 8 or 9 feet approximately for the average office, shelves or cabinets can be added above the files. These extra units have matching door faces which flip up into the unit so that the contents of the drawer/shelf are more easily visible. It is generally recommended not to exceed 6 drawers stacked in combination, with the larger unit on the bottom. More than 6 drawers become difficult to reach or see into, may tip over more easily, and may exceed the structural live load limit of typical office floor construction.

Book shelves and cabinets can either hide or display their contents, depending on whether they have solid doors, glass doors, or no doors at all. Shelving which is factory built can be metal, like the industrial units found in most basements. Shelving and cabinetry can also be finely crafted from rare woods, solid or veneered in combination with more common structural fibre such as plywood or wood pulp process boards. One of the most durable materials for architectural casework, (another name for shelves and cabinets) is plastic laminate, which combines a sophisticated layer of synthetic finish with process wood stock. Contrary to common belief, plastic laminates can create a wide variety of elegant and enchanting accessory constructions to compliment any possible office decor. At the other end of the spectrum, we are all familiar with do-it-yourself shelves made from boards and bricks or concrete blocks. Other masonry units such as clay chimney flue pots, field tile, split face or ribbed blocks, chunks of quarry cut stone or even carefully chosen field stone or sections of logs cut to proper size can provide alternative shelf supports with a less typical appearance. A most unique and delicate effect could be achieved by using thick plate glass shelves supported by 12 inch glass blocks, a trendy designer material these days. Flexibility, durability and clean aesthetics are offered by some manufactured lines of modular storage systems, such as the Haller system. Such a kit uses metal legs, drawer units and metal panels, which can be recombined in an infinite variety of ways.

Most people seem to have a fairly good feeling for the flexibility with which shelves, cabinets and files can serve their activities. Not so the understanding of the basic work station itself, whose form has become some sort of strange tyrant which can never be changed or challenged. It almost seems to be imprinted in the collective unconscious. The principle culprit of this crime against the variety of human need and nature is the ubiquitous

standardized desk, which seems to have been designed for some generic person who works at some generic office. The problems with the basic desk fall into three categories of assumption:
- the size and shape of the work surface;
- the incorporation of storage trays/drawers; and
- the incorporation of equipment.

"The response of many designers to the public as unsophisticated...(follows) the lowest common denominator, rather than the

genuinely felt wants of the consumer."[43]

If the much hailed advent of the customized environment is really going to respond to the diversified needs of "demassified", i.e. unique individuals, there is no better product with which to begin the noble experimentation than the common desk.

As noted above, the answer to the problem lies in separating the desk into its component parts, each of which can then be evaluated and tailored to any given situation on an individual basis.

The first component of the desk is the work surface. The first horizontal work surface was the ground. Later it was discovered that elevated surfaces, such as tree stumps and big rocks relieved one from leaning over so much. The invention of the table should rank right up there with the wheel as evidence of an astounding leap of abstract understanding. Somewhere along the line in the evolution of the table into the desk, we lost track of its principle functions.

The size and shape of a table/desk top are its major assets. These need to relate to both the reach of the arms and the layout space required for the things the arms need to reach, or the space to spread the task objects out in proper relation to each other. A half-donut shape seems to best fit these requirements for maximum reachable surface area. But such desk shapes would threaten to waste precious floor space and also be more expensive to manufacture, which is why they're not readily available.

Instead, most desk tops manufactured today are rectangular in standard sizes, 30 to 36 inches wide with lengths from 5 up to 7 feet. With those sizes and shapes, our ideal half-donut has been straightened out so that it can more easily be pushed into a wall, or out the window. The inability to reach the areas at the far right and left is usually compensated for with chairs that roll on casters. (If your chair doesn't roll, you're in trouble). It seems these desk/table top corners are destined to accumulate accessories and objects which support the activities performed in the central region of the desk/table top, as well as to hold personal icons and memorabilia. This is all a far cry from the first desks we remember in school, those 18 by 24 flip-top units.

The truly critical, functional element of the desk top is that center region which corresponds to the reaching limits of a stationary person. In many cases, the accessories of work would be more easily accomodated on side tables or rolling storage units. Generally, desks would be more usable if they were larger (6' long) or if they were smaller (4' long) and accompanied by side tables. Designers have had to use this sort of arrangement for years because their work surfaces are set at an incline, which causes pencils, pens and coffee cups to become victims of gravity at the blink of an eye.

The second major component of the typical desk is the incorporation of storage. We have already mentioned that the size and shape of desk tops assumes that the upper corners will be used for display and storage. But somewhere back around the days of Louis XIV, someone got a brilliant idea to combine the chest of drawers with the table, and thus the modern desk was born. The problem with the drawers is what to put in them. How do you decide between what goes on top, and what goes inside? Things used most frequently should go on top, but what sort of things don't get used frequently? Do we even need them at all? Most drawers just end up collecting junk, like those so-called "miscellaneous" drawers provided for kitchen cabinet systems. All that metal and money wasted to hold a lot of junk that never gets used.

The worst side effect of these useless bins is the metal or wood skirts or casings which enclose the mechanisms of the drawers. This visual armor makes many desks look like small military vehicles or huge shipping crates. It serves the person protected behind it by hiding the fact of whether or not they have shoes on. Unfortunately, they also restrict one's ability to stretch the legs out straight while sitting at work, which can be annoying.

The third component of the desk is its incorporation of office equipment including telephones, calculators, typewriters and video screen terminals. Since the keyboard units require a different mounting height, relative to standard sitting height, the common approach is to provide a second surface for them. The new finger-touch, air-lift chairs would allow these units to sit atop regular desks while people just changed their seat height when necessary. But that is an unthinkable transgression against the institution of the "typing return", that odd lowered work surface fixed at right angles against one side of the desk or the other. The first problem with the return is that it is usually too small, typically 10 inches wide and 24 inches long, just barely big enough for the typewriter.

The real problem with the return is its inflexibility. Right-handed versus left-handed returns cannot be easily interchanged. This often makes changing furniture arrangements difficult, and it definitely forces the worker to adapt to a fixed situation. The answer would be to return to individual portable stands for different pieces of equipment, which would be quite flexible to change and can be arranged in relation to the principle

work surface and the space.

These of course, need to be more sturdy and stable than those old rickety metal things from the 40's.

The problem of equipment support and accessory storage may best be handled in a sort of wall-unit work storage bar: something substantial with adjustable shelves. Everything should be stored in jars, racks, trays, bins, bowls or whatever to keep it visible and accessible while discouraging private stashes and squirrelling of community property. However, if people insist, drawers and cabinets may still be provided as an option. For the boss who likes a tidy appearance, or for those who wish to insure the confidentiality of their current projects, folding doors or fold-up-type shades would suit the purpose.

The most important aspect of these wall units is that they incorporate storage space above as well as below the work surface/equipment mounting height, and that they have a substantial appearance—not just flimsy racks hanging on moveable partitions. The wall units can be long or short, and can easily function to define the space of individual work stations. Freed of all its extraneous attached elements, the principle desk/work surface can once again become a noble, simple table. It is free to be any material, size, shape, height or position on the floor that is desired. With the adjustable air-lift chair raised to the height of a bar stool, the individual can easily alternate between standing and sitting positions, a great improvement over the status quo.

"Today the consumer who wishes to buy a chair is faced by a bewildering array of 21,336 different models."[44]

The tremendous variety of posture work chairs especially designed for lower back support may be a difficult field from which to choose, unless one desires the air lift option, which is only available currently in a few models. However, the choices in the world of "executive chairs" becomes a rather silly game based on bulkiness and status features rather than flexibility and comfort. Fabric covered seating is generally considered most comfortable and people even prefer it in automobiles, where it may be considered a status item. But when it comes to executive chairs, there is a continued irrational preference for leather or vinyl.

Other critical options chosen for both practical and symbolic reasons are arms, casters, swivel, tilt, and high back. One wonders why they always stop short of going to full La-Z-Boy, preferring instead, to rest the feet on the desk, an ancient act of power and confidence. The tilt option is also good for playing teeter-totter. The whole hassle over who gets what kind of chair can reach such an extreme that, in some cases, the complete hierarchy of a firm can be revealed in the descending order of option complexity; the chair that has everything symbolic at the top, while the chair that has everything truly useful is unwittingly abandoned at the bottom of the pecking order.

It seems that the servants of the individual, both equipment and furniture are best handled as individual components which can be flexibly arranged to meet the changing needs of the work station. All users should carefully consider their true needs, or at least the real complaints they may have against their current work station systems. With an infinite possibility of solutions, only a few could be outlined here to suggest a general approach. There is an army of design professionals around the world who would be more than happy to counsel both organizations and individuals on their real choices for more efficient, comfortable and attractive work stations. The consumer should not be afraid of custom design—initial costs are not as high as generally rumored. And if the designer's first suggestions are over one's budget, then the designer must continue the search and analysis until a proper alternative for the right price is found. For example, the classic alternative to a custom designed work table is a wooden door on saw horses. They even make decorator saw horses these days, in several colors or metallic finishes, on which a plastic laminate top can create an extremely classy appearance for an extremely modest price.

So far in this section, we have discussed the office servants which are easily recognized as discreet objects in space. Now it is time to review those servants which are not tied down to specific points—light, air, sound and, of course, space itself.

The standard office lighting system of flourescent ceiling fixtures seems to be one of the most sophisticated systems for mass psychological torture ever devised. As a friend at a major magazine once said, it is simply impossible for anyone to think clearly for longer than a few hours under the constant eerie glow, which is often accompanied by flickers, buzzes and hums. For many years overzealous lighting engineers promoted the idea that absolutely every point on the whole office floor should be evenly illuminated to the maximum level, which is both silly and wasteful. They could think only in terms of lumens per square foot.

In recent years, designers, engineers and manufacturers have begun to explore the only reasonable alternative, known as task/ambient lighting systems. Ambient means the general overall space lighing, which is kept at a low level, bright enough to see for moving around the space, but not bright enough by which to perform visual work tasks. Ambient lighting is usually indirect, which means that it is bounced off of the walls or ceilings. Most people agree that it has a very pleasant effect. The task lighting elements are provided at each work station. The best kind are those which have adjustable levels of brightness, and adjustable positions. This allows for actual energy savings, since individuals would only use as much as they need, when they need it.

Since we all prefer the soft and subtle varieties of natural light, this is the best source of ambient lighting, if the room/space layout permits sunlight penetration to all areas of the office floor. A very ingenuous architect recently developed a marvelous window system that scoops in an unusually large amount of light and bounces it far back into the space. Besides being very pleasant, this kind of light is also free. Proper blinds, shading devices or reflective glass can reduce or eliminate glare and heat gain. For the task lights, the general preference for incandescant rather than flourescent lights is due to both the real as well as the imagined qualities of the light. Unfortunately, flourescent lighting suffers from the negative connotations of our first associations between it and the garage or the basement.

Air is the servant without which none of us can survive, let alone work. Fresh air at the correct temperature seems to be a luxury that even the most powerful executives find difficult to gain. Over-reliance on mechanical ventilation systems for office buildings eliminated the operable window for two reasons —to simplify programming of mechanical units and also to eliminate the extra cost of the window itself. In temperate climates, the period of change between the warm and cold season seems just as impossible for these mechanical wonders to handle as it is natural for someone to just open the window to let the mild, fresh air blow through. One thinks the energy savings by using such a natural system would more than offset any expense or inconvenience when the windows are opened at less opportune times of the year.

Especially in offices where many people smoke, the staleness of the air seems almost bad enough to destroy brain cells. Air-handling systems always seem to provide too much or too little. Anyone lucky enough to sit right under the diffuser seems doomed to constant head colds and sore necks. Everyone else has to bring in portable fans so they can breath and/or stay cool. Some locations near windows during the winter can get so cold, people have to bring in space heaters.

To be sure, the relationships between the building skin system, mechanical ventilating systems, changing weather conditions and the wide variety of individual preferences are unbelievable complicated. We can be sure that trying to handle the situation on a global basis for entire floors is totally ridiculous and inadequate. Experimentation with small zone responsive systems have been going on for several years, but they have a long way to go before we reach the ideal situation, which we already have for lighting systems, of individually controlled air/temperature supply networks that are at least as comfortable and efficient as the spot under a shady tree on top of a breezy hill. Well, we can always dream.

Another reason for which operable windows on office buildings were eliminated was the need to control noise. Each advance of technology seems to add new character to the generally inescapable nature of noise pollution. For offices located close to busy streets, this problem may continue to prohibit the use of operable windows. But for most other offices, the audio environment is internally created and therefore internally controlled.

Similar to the problem of correcting typewritten material,

there are two basic solutions—to eliminate the unwanted elements or else cover them up. Sources of noise in the office can be machines or people or both. Many devices are available to reduce or eliminate machine noise on a unit by unit basis— collecting the noise makers into discrete areas and screening or shutting them off from the rest of the office. The universal method of noise control which may be used in combination with all of these other techniques involves sound absorbing materials for ceiling, floor and wall surfaces. We are all familiar with acoustical tile ceilings. Fortunately the unsightly exposed supporting grids can now be eliminated at a slightly extra expense in favor of concealed spline systems. Carpeting on the floor also absorbs a lot of noise.

Beyond these typical applications, significant improvements can be made by using sound absorbing panels as vertical partitions dividing the office space. These fabric or carpet-covered units filled with sound absorbing material are the reason many open offices are actually quieter than typical offices with hard-surfaced floor to ceiling walls, even when everyone has their doors shut.

The cover-up solution to noise can involve piped-in music or low level random sounds, known as white noises, to mask the distracting elements of the audio environments. Many offices even allow individual control of this with personal desk radios. The ultimate solution of headphones and tape cassettes unfortunately also eliminates one's exposure to the daily informal flow of events and information that is actually not

noise

but a vital part of collective office operations. When the general sounds provide their own cover up, we experience the natural conditions of the cafe, which is both open and private at the same time.

Space itself seems to be the most slippery subject of all. The work space can be used in a wide variety of ways. Our point here is that space is a three-dimensional arena for work in which all the other servants of work become unified and coordinated with each other, according to the needs of the individual, the team and the organization.

Space is the stage which is brought to life by the people and things which occupy it and articulate it. The same 3-dimensional volume can take on a totally different character or atmosphere according to its many variables:

— POWER   115

- different people or things can occupy it;

- the same people or things can occupy it in different ways or arrangements;

- the boundary or enclosure may have a uniform, constant nature; or

- the boundary or enclosure may have a variable nature, possibly including openings or views into other spaces, or illusions of extension by mirrors, etc.

As mentioned earlier the human characteristic of feeling the bubble of space around us to be an extension of our bodies and ourselves. The definition or boundary of this space bubble can be created in a wide variety of ways, each of which can have many side effects on the character and quality of the work station. Besides the typical fixed floor-to-ceiling walls and movable accoustical panel systems, another possibility is the use of actual drapes and curtains, which can run on tracks integrated with the ceiling systems, fire codes permitting. The top 10 inches of the drapes could be open netting to allow the free flow of light and air. But the rest of the drapes down to the floor would provide a high degree of sound absorption. Besides offering a much wider variety of color, pattern and texture than current movable partition systems, the drapes also return to the individual the opportunity to "close the door" by drawing them to a closed position. The overall effect of such an office system could be both enchanting and exciting.

POWER:
Muses

"...rituals over time leave their impressions on the walls and forms of the interior and endow the rooms with artifacts which give us access to previous experience...the centerplaces in the house are the regions where the memories of the self can be ritualized and new memories belonging to the family (i.e. or the firm) can be accumulated and experienced..."[45]

The power of the muses as an indirect or oblique aid to the processes of office work, lie in their ability to:

- remind us of the data and criteria which are the object of our operations (i.e. maps of sales districts, work duty assignments, calculation tables, production schedules, etc.);

- reaffirm the values and principles which guide our actions or the style in which we operate (i.e. honesty, ruthlessness, courtesy, thoroughness, etc.);

- stimulate the creation of ideas or solutions to problems by the suggestive power of the rich associations we perceive;

- generate energy through their contribution to a pleasant, positive general task environment.

Muses affect the visitors to an office, as well as the inhabitants. Muses are not just for amusement.

In the first chapter, we followed a lengthy discussion of the subconsious, irrational holistic mind/body activities which are an important element of almost anything done at the office. Fantasy, memory, daydream, ritual, creativity and play all can enhance the daily flow of data transformation and human exchange, for both pleasure and profit. Our actual physical environment must reinforce all possible sources of energy and ideas, or else the magic will leak out through the gaps and be gone forever. Each passing moment should be optimized, as any efficiency expert might say.

Information display has already been mentioned several times. When it directly serves the task at hand, it is a servant. But when its relation to task is indirect or general, it is a muse. The best example is a wall-sized map of the world, 8 feet high by 13 feet long. The international executive can use it directly to locate the unfamiliar city of a new project or to spot the position of the associate on the other end of a long distance phone call. Contemplating the map is a constant reminder of the corporation's frontiers and of all the activities progressing along them. Besides all of that, it's really a beautiful thing to look at; bold, dynamic blue ocean shapes separated by elegant land forms in shaded contours and etched in a lacework of rivers and place names. Visitors are always fascinated by it.

Other muses of this sort include the company logo or insignia, awards, citations, certificates, human anatomy drawings, periodic charts of the chemical elements, terrestrial and interterrestrial maps of all scales and types, organizational performance diagrams, lists of goals, the company motto, and in fact anything for which we need a bulletin board, black board, paper tablet on an easel, or just a push pin stick in the wall. Magazines, books and dictionaries are muses, too.

Most muses, however, are very personal. Diplomas proclaim our academic degrees to impress others as well as to remind us of our abilities and responsibilities. Calendars, appointment books, time cards and work diaries help us to organize our time and develop priorities. Sometimes the calendar works like a guardian angel, preventing certain confusion and disaster if everything was left to memory or not planned at all.

But calendars can also be a conspicuous display with a monthly variety of images from fields of wild flowers to pin-up girls or boys. Calendars function as marketing ambassadors when they are given as gifts to clients and customers.

In general, anything which serves the office operation can also be a muse if it is inspiring to use. "Many products already successfully embody values of high associational context."[46] It is more fun to type on an elegant keyboard, or talk into a classy telephone. When we enjoy doing something, we probably do it better. Status games aside, this may be the reason so much emphasis is placed on the choice of personal chairs. The style of the chair can say a lot about the person in it. A chair can make us feel special, like a throne. We can develop such a close relationship with our chair, that it seems to be part of our body, as if we were office-centaurs, half human and half chair. Like the centaur's equine torso, the chair is also our vehicle. The chair defines our most intimate domain as it sets the tone of our daily activity.

All sorts of personal objects and artifacts create secondary patterns and layers of associational richness that personalize the task environment and enhance our energy and productivity. Family photos and plants are the most usual touches of home, reminders of the reasons why we are here in the office in the first place. The mounted trophy fish gazes down from the wall. The child's crayon masterpiece smiles up from beside the phone. The private collections include mementos, good luck charms, and icons of inspiration ranging from graduation tassels, pipes, and honorarium desk pen sets, to famous framed "first dollar ever earned". Anything from nature can be a muse: a soft sunrise or twinkling stars, a fountain or a crackling fire, smells of every sort, views of the mountain or the sea, shells and coral, rocks and driftwood, and of course flowers. Even fish or birds or animals can enter the office, for far more than decorative effect.

Man-made works of art, from machine parts and views out over a city to fine paintings, are an obvious source of pleasure and inspiration in the office. Whatever the material from which the piece is made, or the message intended by the artist, we continue to find new associations in the piece as we see it day after day. Art can be a mirror by which we come to understand ourselves, as well as one which can speak to us, suggesting answers to the problems which we confront. Most of all, works of art, whether they are religious or not, are a direct source of energy in proportion to the intensity of effort by which they were made. That is why a great work of art, from a fantastic print to a fabulous car, can give you the shivers; you know the maker has put a bit of his

soul

into the piece.

The muse of the human spirit feeds on itself. The great scholar of Indian religious art, Dr. Kramrisch, has explained this function in terms of the image of shiva; "...The consecrated image provides the means by which the devotee identifies with the divinity that resides in the image... Indian art neither depicts iconographic themes or mythical motives, nor does it illustrate allegories..." Instead, the contemplated object is considered murti, "the concrete shape of an invisible inner realization of a transcendand vision. It is the body in which the god is made real"[47]

Decorative art works for the office include paperweight collections, stained glass, tapestries, rugs, paintings, sculpture, archeological fragments, photos, drawings and perhaps even a television which may be more reasonably described as an electronic pet. All of these muses can have a profound effect on the office place and process.

Most of the muses mentioned so far are agents of the external environment. There are, of course, those muses which are experienced internally. Light waves tickle our nerves through our eyes just as sound waves do through our ears, but you can't touch music with your fingers. Audio stimulation tends to have a more immediate emotional and physical impact than visual stimulation, which must often work its effects through our mental perceptions and thinking processes. Paintings don't make you tap your feet. Lucky are those whose favorite tunes can blend in with the daily office routine. The psychologist Singer explains that "the definite psychological values of music lie, not so much in the encouragement of inner directed orientation as in the very direct physical, perceptual, aesthetic response..."[48] However, this muse taken to an extreme can be a demon, so it is nice to get real peace and quiet sometimes, or at least to change the radio station occasionally.

The last big group of office muses are the things we actually put into our bodies. How many cups of coffee have been poured in the name of commerce? How many cocktails, jugs of wine, gallons of Tab, loaves of bread or cherry danish or onion bagels have been consumed by the office community?

POWER:
Paraphernalia

"Il n'importe qu'on vive, mais comment." It matters not that we live, but how." "A thing of beauty may have no practical use, a thing of use, no appreciable beauty, but in their union the creative genius of man finds its highest and divinest expression."[49]

As the Chinese philosopher Lao Tzu has said, the world is filled with ten thousands of things. And so, too, the office is filled with thousands of devices and gadgets which are the accessories of work. No matter how humble, from pencils to paper clips, their physical appearance can either add to, or subtract from the overall office image. As mentioned earlier, well-made objects can be more enjoyable to use, and probably work better and last longer. Good quality office accessories should be chosen whenever the budget allows.

The legions of office paraphenalia seem endless:

- paperweights
- letter openers
- letterhead stationary
- oversized envelopes
- tablet paper
- toilet paper
- memo pads
- preprinted forms
- sticky labels
- file folders with hangers and tabs
- wooden pencils

TRANSFORMING YOUR OFFICE

- automatic pencils
- felt tip pens
- technical, fountain and ballpoint pens
- tape and tape dispensers
- glue
- stapler and staple remover
- paper clips and paper clip holder
- scissors
- paper cutters
- waste baskets
- pencil holders
- Rolodex
- in/out trays
- rubber bands
- typing ribbons and elements
- press-on letters
- report covers and brochure binders
- rulers
- pencil sharpeners
- postal scales and meters
- vacuum cleaners
- robot delivery systems
- coffee makers
- refrigerators
- vending machines
- sinks
- grills and micro-wave ovens
- cups, dishes, flatware and glasses
- spiral punch machines
- 2-hole and 3-hole punches
- mirrors
- flags
- waterbeds
- jacuzis
- saunas
- fireplaces
- pin ball machines
- pool tables
- etc.

POWER:
Things As A Whole

Somehow all of the functions of people and things, of individuals, teams, organizations, servants, muses, and paraphernalia must be brought together as whole. As we have seen, there is a tremendous number of variables and choices to consider. All too often, things get thrown together in an ad hoc, expedient manner, with little thought about actual usefulness.ss. Without good components, the resulting whole may be less than satisfactory. That doesn't mean that everything necessarily has to be the ritz. It just means that things should be chosen which fit together, as well as fit the needs of the user. A whole is something integrated, unified, and greater than the sum of its parts.

The path of choices towards a really useful office set-up must begin with the basic issues of information and organization. To these are added the needs and desires of the individual people involved, and the teams in which they operate. As the office begins to take shape, there is an expression of values, style, or image which should guide the choice of every piece of furniture, equipment, and accessories.

Beyond that point, the process of personal habitation takes over, bringing the office to life. As long as the basic original concepts have been maintained in the developement of office layout, the sense of order should always prevail over the possible chaos of individualized work stations. In a thoughtfully arranged office, no matter how informal, fears of disorder are not justified. There may be many voices in the chorus, but they will sing the same song.

Closing this chapter is a very specific description of a complete personal work station. Though the user is a student, and therefore does not require access and exposure to organizational teammates, the issue of "things as a whole" is well conveyed: "The maturing student wants his privacy, his special place. We have learned by experimental work in education at Southern Illinois University of the I.Q. capability favoring that was attainable with (an individual space) which belonged to each student. When he first entered he found in his (personal space) all kinds of desireable items. He had his own telephone directly and privately connected to his teacher. He found a good dictionary;

wall charts of the periodic table of the elements; a world globe; a wall mounted chart of the electromagnetic spectrum; his private typewriter; and other items conducive to thought and study. He did not feel inclined to go out of that room in order to find an environment more favorable to study. However he was not allowed to go into that room unless he was going to study... The student found that when he was in his private study, his reflexes became

progressively conditioned by association with that environment

to give himself spontaneously to study, calculation, and writing. He found himself producing. His mind really began to work."[50]

"You can't always get what you want, but it you try sometimes, you might find you get what you need."[51]

The needs of the office are many. The answer to them is found in ergonomics; ergon meaning work, nomos meaning law. Everything we have discussed is in some way required or needed in the optimum work process. These things involve all of the physical, psychological, and sociological aspects of man and his task environment. The most important ergonomic principle, the container of the ten thousand things and activities at the office, is the "sense of place" holistically integrated, to enhance a greater awareness of the simple rituals of life and work, bringing positive effects through all sensual modalities.

THREE
PLACE

PLACE:
Models, Symbols and Attributes

"Dr. Einstein did not sit in the middle of Grand Central Station in order best to study...he went into seclusion."[1]

"... habitats should present a model of the cosmos and the self simultaneously, so that the resident can feel centered and in balance with his universe..."[2]

The elusive qualities which make the difference between a work space and a work place are based on energy and values associated with elements of the environment. Attitudes regarding space, nature, habitat and human behavior are as different between the east and the west as are the related symbols, languages and aesthetics. Many westerners are easily infatuated by the mysteries of the Orient to the extent that we sometimes overlook or forget some of the intriguing paradoxes of our own culture. It may be a good idea to attempt understanding ourselves first, as a basis for understanding others.

In the U.S., our habitat begins with the natural landscape which was subdivided by the national survey grid to provide the framework for future identification and development. This planning grid, as universal and impersonal as the modular building grids of the modern architect Mies van der Rohe, is in itself, neither sacred nor profane.[3] In Thomas Jefferson's time, this grid came to symbolize the society which it made possible — the utopian agrarian communities of the expanding frontier.

The belief at the time was that rural environments produced more virtuous citizens, because the economic structure of rural society, i.e. between the independent farms, allows "proper" relations between men. This was in contrast to the city where men were more likely to cause trouble through debts and other legal entanglements of business. Since the city has always been associated with culture and learning, the intellectuals who thrived on city life came to be as mistrusted as the city itself.

It is an American trait to seek the proverbial pot of gold at the end of the rainbow, and the city has promised fame and fortune to young people of every generation. The suburb, as originally imagined in the period of the Reconstruction following the Civil War, could combine the best of both worlds — peace, quiet, clean air, safety, and detached single family dwellings, with wide green lawns (the essence of the rural life), as well as access to fame, fortune, shops and the cultural excitements of the city. One would be able to escape the bad elements of both worlds — the boredom of the country and the evil dangers of the city. This is the foundation of the traditional American sense of place.

The general attitude of western civilization was founded in the Renaissance; the great culture awakening in Europe which began almost 500 years ago. We are all familiar with the figures of Leonardo da Vinci and Michelangelo, great multi-talented artists who were model Renaissance men. The beginning of the Age of Humanism brought an end to the medieval piety and humility of mankind the face of cosmic order. Instead, we assumed a place at the center of the universe, "a precarious position we seek constantly to justify our search for history, community and permanence..."[4] Sir Kenneth Clark has rather neatly explained that, "The birth of civilization depends on confidence..."[5] Moore and Bloomer maintain that "...Our beings must be centered — the house/self must be at the center axis of the infinite cosmos..."[6]

Monuments and landmarks are traditional tools for differentiating the environment and for orienting ourselves. A landscape without "noticeable, significant monuments, expressing shared cultural values, is incomplete...truly folk landscapes are composed of both temporary utilitarian and permanently symbolical elements..."[7] It is easy to see how the drinking fountain or water cooler in today's office may also be thought of as a monument in the landscape/cityscape of the office. If the function of an element is important to office operation, it too may be honored with spatial significance.

Models for different kinds of places can come from nature, society, myths and literature. Models from nature include islands and beaches, forests and hills, pinnacles and mesas, grottos and canyons, rivers and oceans, etc. Models from society include hearth, throne, tower, garret, cellar, shrine, grove, oasis, burial place, wall, gate, etc. The old saying that "a man's home is his castle" employs this idea of the place model.

The farm, the working landed estate, provides an excellent model of a place/process relationship similar to an office. An unusual example of myth providing a model or guideline for the image of place may be found at Frank Lloyd Wright's home in Wisconsin. The house, called Taliesin, was built into the landscape in order to form the "shining brow" of the hilltop as a reflection of the Celtic myth of the famous poet with the "shining brow". Since young Wright heard these and many other tales from his Welsh grandfather, he was able to weave other celtic images of forest, hill and burial place into the fabric of his design.[8] Other mythical models of place include Olympus, Atlantis, and the Emerald City in the Land of Oz.[9]

Since ancient times the mountain has been the symbol of a place of special inspiration. In the Old Testament of the Bible, Moses receives God's law in a meeting on the sacred mountain. In Spencer's '**Fairie Queen**' the hero of the allegory sees a vision of the Celestial City from a mountaintop. There are hundreds of similar stories. The mountain is a "tower of power," and the stone of which the mountain is made is magical too. John Brinkerhoff Jackson has given an excellent dissertation on the energy and values associated with man's all time favorite building material, stone. Stones are fragments from the fiery birth of our planet. They are our parents, linking us to the stars, our ancestors. Stone carries powerful significance because of its oldness. It is the ultimate symbol of indestructible reality, even though its erosion by wind and water can also symbolize the greater power of time and change.[10]

Stone used in building carries great emotional impact. The special appearance connotes high status, strength, power, wealth, etc. The precision engineering and the sheer work of moving great masses of stone is suggestive of magic. The manner in which the great blocks of stone were moved to build the pyramids in Egypt still remains a mystery.

Henry Hobson Richardson, an American architect, raised the level of architectural stonework and masonry to an art in the last quarter of the nineteenth century. "Richardson freely used the heavy stone and geometric simplicity of the Romanesque style as a fitting expression of American industrial life."[11] This tremendous period of activity is best described by the sensitive historian, Vincent Scully:

"With Richardson, American architecture entered its mythic phase: mythic itself, more or less consciously, in its content; mythic surely in the historical significance which what might be called the present American Studies generation has assigned to it. Brooklyn Bridge can mark its beginning. The towers are still mid-century Gothic, sharp and linear, but the roadway sweeps out into the new continuity of space which was to be the salient feature of the architecture of Richardson, Sullivan and Wright, and hence America's major contribution to the first phases of international modern architecture in the early twentieth century. The bridge itself towered over the city; the curve of its road cut high above the old buildings. So it introduced all at once the scale of a new urban world and released into space its symbol of the roadway rushing continuously onward. It is no wonder that the bridge, with its taut, singing cables, was to gain increasing force as an image of all America as the twentieth century wore on. Hart Crane gave it everything:

'O sleepless as the river under thee,
Vaulting the sea, the prairies' dreaming sod...'"[12]

Among the architects of this time was Louis Sullivan, the last great celebrant of Humanism, before world culture made the technological shift. Like every great architect before him, he tried to build on the best traditions of the works of his peers and predecesors. Sullivan admired Richardson for the ability to "fuse borrowed and invented forms (and ornaments) into a truly homogeneous, dynamic whole whose many parts are rationally subordinate, one to another, in accordance with their function."[13] Sullivan also admired 'The Rookery' by John Wellborn Root.[14] The heavy, rough yet carefully assembled red granite blocks are in counterpoint with the large smooth transparent glass areas and the luciously wrought ornamentations.

"Root's expressive unity, worked out in a romantic interplay of dualities served Sullivan well in his own attempts to establish a harmonious accord between the external appearance of things and their inner experience."[15]

Sullivan wanted ornamental architecture to become a vehicle to raise people and their habitat above the common level of materialism. His goals were right in step with the writings of Ralph Waldo Emerson, and other Transcendentalists. "The expressive range of Sullivan's ornament extends from clarification of simple, structural elements to suggestion of mystical, cosmic forces."[16] For example, the arch was for Sullivan symbolic of the acceptance and transcendance of death. He called it

"a form against fate"

and used it most appropriately at the entrance portal of his celebrated Stock Exchange.[17] It was Sullivan's greatest desire "to transform utility into transcendant metaphor."[18]

This transcendental idea was also the seed of the modern aesthetic revolution. The ground for this seed was tilled by M. Samuel Bing, the Paris art exhibiter who invented the term "Art Nouveau" as the name for his gallery. "It was simply the name of an establishment opened as a meeting ground for all ardent young spirits anxious to manifest the modernness of their tendencies, and open also to all lovers of art who desired to see the working of the hitherto unrevealed forces of our day..."[19] Bing selected works for his gallery according to two basic principles: "Each article to be strictly adapted to its proper purpose; Harmonies to be sought for in lines and colour."[20] "It was necessary to resist the mad idea of throwing off all

associations with the past."[20]

The surest path for the artist, architect or citizen in general, according to Bing, was to do nothing "more than take up the work at the point where his predecessor had left it, and in his turn develop it logically to meet the general spirit of the age in which he was living."[21]

"In the wide field now open each of us can sow his seed according to the fruits he wishes to gather...crude imitations, shaped without regard to the most elementary rules of logic...prevent hesitating spirits from seeing that the time has come for us to shake off our foolish inertia and that there is now no longer any reason why our decorative arts should not recover their full freedom of expansion and flourish as gloriously as they did in former times."[22] "The idea that Bing expressed, that Beauty might reside in a form created to solve a complex practical need was truly modern."[23]

To unsympathetic eyes, the work of Sullivan and his associates appeared otherwise. Henrik Berlage, a German architect favoring a more brutal aesthetic claimed that the New Free Style of original ornamentation was "created to gratify the taste for novelty and escape of a wealthy, carefree aristocracy; the movement of an eclectic, ever-changing age that injects criticism into its art. Stunning fantasy of a cosmopolitan art, artificial, brilliant improvisation that responds to the fever and paroxysm of the moment."[24]

The New Free Style and the Arts and Crafts Movement in general did not survive the cultural purge of the Machine Age and the related socialist political movements. Sullivan, as the most sensitive genius of the doomed was like his arch, "form against fate." He sowed the seeds of his own destruction with his call for an "honest" architecture, which unfortunately was carried out in only the most material fashion.[25] Perhaps this message can be heard today in its original, full sense, to kindle the next wave of the evolution of the human environment.

Everyone is familiar with where this evolution has brought us today. Once the initial shock of the new high technology buildings wore off, the public witnessed in disbelief the steady invasion and eventual dominance of glass boxes. Their coldness and sterility repulsed those who could not appreciate the refined levels of conceptual elegance in minimal art; which is to say almost everybody. The people turned back to the warm, dark hulking urban blocks that had survived the wrecking balls. These were places that could be experienced emotionally because they were so obviously touched by the hands of men, as well as by their minds.

Buildings and places in general can and should make people feel good. Places of power, such as governements and businesses feel a necessity to impress people. Unfortunately, this has been effected with negative results of fear and repression or boredom and depression, rather than the positive results of joy and celebration of the wonder of man, civilization, and life. Certainly the marvels and beauties of science celebrate man also, but perhaps they are more appropriate to the high flying space shuttle than to earthbound buildings.[26] In the golden age of the skyscraper it was the symbol of man's spirit to soar beyond the confines imposed by nature. Now that a new symbol carries that message it seems most urgent that habitat honestly addresses the real needs of real people, not just the ones on T.V.

Similarly, the subtle mysteries of minimal art are an undeniably great achievement, in which the connoussieurs delight. But it is inappropriate to impose such places on the general population, who perceive them as both alien and insane. Nevertheless, such places are still preferable to the unbelievable junk comprising the lion's share of construction today, perpetuated by insensitive or weak-kneed developers and designers.

And the greatest part of this is for offices.

It is no wonder that the human spirit seems to be going down the tubes. And yet, all of this is an organizing response to the evolution of the habitat development process. What was once guided by kings and men of vision is now dominated by investors and bankers who can only appreciate beauty in financial figures.

Where artisans and laborers once took tremendous individual satisfaction along with their wages as the reward for work, unions now plan only for the strategies to engineer their next pay hikes, rather than how to improve the level of their craft and productivity. The whole mess is like a giant snowball crashing down the hill, an avalanche that can crush us all. There are no special interests; everyone must respond in a personal way to the crisis of our habitat. Everyone must care.

Sometimes the environment seems to be alive. Places can have powers and personalities that act on the people who reside there.[27] Such places as Southfork Ranch in Dallas, or Sunset Boulevard in Hollywood, or Old Sante Fe in New Mexico have a sense of being, a sense that they might exist with or without our attention to them.

On the scale of individual buildings, Richardson's were often like fantastic creatures, "The tiny railroad station at Chestnut Hill, Massachusetts, is an insatiable monster, swallowing up vehicles...Bruce Price's Osborne Hall at Yale, where the arches writhed back from short columns like teeth, sucking in and spewing out the stairs like Charybdis the sea..."[28] This idea is the basis for the gothic horror tales of haunted houses. Sullivan sought to breath life into the places he made, "to vitalise building materials, to animate them with a thought, a state of feeling, to charge them with a subjective significance and value, to make them a visible part of the social fabric, to infuse into them the life of the people, as the eye of the poets..."[29] His deepest belief was that the places of our habitat, our homes and our offices, "should carry man from physical or sensual elegance and richness to higher transcendent states of awareness."[30]

Coming back down to earth, the proper groundwork has been prepared on which to discuss the types of office places currently and potentially available. If the reader can keep in mind the concepts and issues outlined up to this point, and the few that are yet to come, he may find himself discovering all sorts of ideas to use in improving the office as both a place and a process. That is the reward of new understanding. The curse will be the frustrations along the road to realizing these new ideas, but is there really any choice? That which does not continue to grow and adapt is doomed to perish.

PLACE:
Location

Undeniably, the most influential aspect of an office location is the climate. The responsive variations of office form, organization and image are so obviously limited by the local weather that we usually take them for granted. It would be impossible to adequetely cover this vast topic in the scope of this book. However, keep the issue of climate in the back of your mind while we examine urban, suburban/exurban, and rural/mobile office locations.

The original and still principle location for offices is the city. The basic question "What makes a city?" commonly evokes the response "It's a noisy, crowded, dirty, dangerous, expensive place to live...but its the only place I can get a job, or get paid for not working..."; in other words, the cesspool of civilization. Others have answered the question in a different way. Lewis Mumford emphasizes the city's original features as a haven of safety, a focus of power, a storehouse, a center of trade and learning, the synthesis of interelated cultural elements. The city is a place of special energy and resource for the simple fact that so many people are there, and so closely connected. That is why New York can never die. "The city performed its special function — that of a complex receptacle for maximizing the possibilities of human intercourse and passing on the contents of civilization..."[31]

Bringing people together is a primary urban function. The device for doing this is public space: streets, squares, parks, plazas, lobbies, elevators, subways, alleys, cafes, galleries, etc. These conduits of circulation blend into the domain of private enterprise, frequented by both clients and staff. In other words, every office is a node of the network of the urban movement system.

How you get a place is a big part of the experience of that place. Edmund Bacon points out, "Movement through space creates a continuity of experience derived from the nature and form of the spaces through which the movement occurs."[32] Office experience can be different on the days that we walk or bicycle to work from the days that we ride the bus or take a taxi. "The procession was not primarily to provide a spectacle for the onlooker, but rather to create an event in which many could take part...architectural effort was directed toward providing punctuating points in the experience...(which includes) the way people clothe themselves and their awareness of the changing role of their garments in relation to the background."[33] The environmental framework and the pageant it contains are inseperable.[34]

This containment, this boundary definition and directional focus, is the most important feature of urban space — not size or decoration. This principle is well remembered when the office space is organized. Rob Krier, an Austrian architect, has studied in detail the infinite possible combinations of the street and the square. He claims, "It is only the clear legibility of its geometrical characteristics and aesthetic qualities which allow us to consciously perceive external space as urban space."[35] In such a case, space is a positive element, that is, it has a definite shape. When buildings are disconnected and unrelated to objects along a street and the space has no boundaries or shape at all, then it is a negative element. Such terms don't imply good or bad necessarily, it just means that in the case of a positive element, we sense the force of a presence, something is there. In the case of a negative element, we sense it only as a background against which we can read the presence of other things, like the outlines of fence posts against the sky.

Within the city, a wide range of possible office locations are available to every size firm, at different costs varying with ease of access, visibility and prestige. The classic locations in the heart of the downtown, central business districts (CBD's) are along a broad tree lined boulevard, or facing across the street to a park. Office buildings may front on a square or they can create their own small plaza by being set back from the street. Office buildings can also be at the end of a street terminating the long, grand perspective, axial view, or they can be the focus of a busy corner. Irregular street grid patterns, like the winding, narrow thoroughfares found in Europe, Boston and San Francisco, may offer a more romantic or mysterious office location.

Similar atmosphere and ambience may be found on a side street or tucked away down an alley. The current waves of renovation and redevelopment of the transition areas surrounding the CBD's gains its momentum as much from the desire for the alternative environment found in old warehouse and industsrial loft buildings as from the economics of the situation and the proximity to downtown services and supports.[36]

Beyond these transition areas, the busy streets of the urban neighborhoods offer storefront spaces for offices, in a community atmosphere that can be more personal as well as more practical, depending on the office needs. This situation is quite similar to the traditional

Main Street

still found all over this country in small towns. A few other unique locations for the office in the city may be on a pier or boat dock, on or under a bridge or even in a tunnel. For all these cases, the office could be the entire building, a whole floor, or a room off a corridor — from the basement to the penthouse.

There is a special opportunity for offices which can occupy a whole house or townhouse. This trend is most popular in areas of large, older homes close to the business districts of small cities and large towns.

The options for an office within an urban residence are rooms, or spaces within rooms carved out of highrise apartments, grand old blocks of European style flats, or low rise townhouses. The study corner in a bedroom, or a full fledged library can be equally useful if they are thoughtfully organized. The greatest challenge is the one room studio apartment which must also double as an office. These can take advantage of the many tricks used in convertible hotel suites, from Murphy beds and fold out sofas to shelves hidden behind cabinet doors. The only limitation is one's imagination. An old trunk can double as a coffee table and typing return when put next to a desk. The desk could be a hollow core door resting on top of stereo speakers. A round dining table provides an alternative work station and a setting for conferences, complimented by a bookcase with glass doors which can double as a credenza or buffet server.

Preconceptions concerning possible uses for different things is the biggest barrier to making fun out of functions.

The line dividing suburban zones from urban neighborhoods is hard to pin down, but suburban characteristics of low density and chaotic space flowing around isolated buildings signals the boundary.

The patchwork quilt of parking lots in many medium sized cities has actually changed urban space into suburban space. The other major feature of the suburban environment is the priority given to the automobile over the pedestrian. This is, in fact, the leading cause of the spaced-out building patterns. Cities which were built mostly after World War Two, like Los Angeles or Phoenix exhibit this arrangement. Exurban office buildings are a familar sight scattered throughout the new American landscape, like spots of a certain color in an "intricately designed, mass-produced wall-paper."[37] The spots range in quality from the banal and bombastic to the elegant and exciting. Wherever and however the spots are built, they stand as physically and psychically isolated from each other as the spots of the surrounding suburban houses. Each world is a private self-defined society.

In spite of the seeming variety of types constructed, office buildings often appear very similar. As corporations struggle for distinction in the corporate world/exurban landscape, they usually sink into the anonymity created by that very struggle, just as the establishments along the commercial strip become anonymous in their struggle for visual impact. The passing motorist may only get a general impression of the collage as a whole.

Exurban office buildings are typically located near an interstate or state highway, due to ease of access and high visibility. Sites near the intersections of such roads can be more constricted than sites along the sides. Roadway sites post rather interesting orientation problems because actual access to the site may be from a frontage road on the opposite side of the lot from the main road, which has better commercial exposure. Which facade should become "the front", and where to place parking, entry and service areas depend on the operations and image needed by the particular business. Another variant for roadway location with good visibility is along the access road to the highway interchange from an established area of activity such as small business districts and regional malls, or between two centers of activity. Major state and country roads which connect regional shopping centers are a very popular place for office development, especially speculative projects. The pattern resembles the mall scheme itself: the shopping centers generate intense circulation on axis and insure the commercial exposure of the establishments between them.

Another familiar pattern of exurban office development is the office park. It is call a "park" for one or more of the following reasons:

- it incorporates large, landscaped areas;
- its cul-de-sac road systems has only one access point to a major street, preventing through traffic; and
- its internal roads curve like the winding drives through a park.

Sometimes the parks include both industrial and office buildings. A developer may create a park complete with buildings or provide only the intrastructure of roads and utilities so that individual corporations or builders can develop their own lots. "A common problem with office parks has been a scattered building effect where it is difficult to achieve individual distinction and where the outdoor areas are amorphous — neither having the containment of urban development or the openness of rural spaces."[38] In all of these cases the buildings are isolated objects.

Some general guidelines for making the most of a roadway site evolved through the experimentations of fast food and other franchise operations, whose survival totally depends on visibility and access. Everything along the strip is subordinate to the road. The view of the driver is focused ahead as he moves along, a relatively passive being inside a machine through which he senses and responds to the road. Consequently, hills, dips and turns where changes command the driver's attention, offer the best opportunities for visual contact.[39]

One's sense of speed is greatly affected by the interrelation of the width of the road and the size and spacing of elements along it. Apparent speed decreases as the road widens and/or roadside objects are set further back. Apparent speed increases as the opposite things occur. Because of the speed of passing motorists, signage and architectural features of roadside buildings must be larger and more clearly defined in order to call attention and convey information, compared to buildings which people pass at a much slower pace, such as walking downtown. This is because the increase in speed narrows the field of vision and shifts attention from details to generalities.

Suburbia does not offer as wide a range of office locations as the city. Storefronts are on the strip and tend to be miniature corporate headquarters in a noisy area. Nearly 100 percent of suburban offices are speculative buildings or private facilities of recent construction.

The suburb does offer a much greater variety of offices in the home because there is more space. In addition to the study corner, library or desk built in with kitchen cabinetry, new spatial opportunities can be explored in the basement, attic, garage and coach house. The most recent craze in the home office scene is to attach a greenhouse/sun room to the south side of the house. With correct installation, there can be an energy tax credit, (40 percent in 1980.)

The standard rural location for office buildings is a large isolated site, usually in beautiful country. Such elitist retreats are best suited for corporate headquarters because their cost and seclusion can connote the prestige of a baronial estate. Due to the size of the site and building budget, these headquarters can take advantage of a wider variety of design alternatives than other offices.

Opportunities for rural and wilderness offices may be found in a barn or resort or hotel complex. A small operation may fit perfectly into a farmhouse or log cabin. Of course, this presents the problem of employee access. But with the ever advancing state of communications technology, such peaceful surroundings will become increasingly practical for operations which require concentration and relaxation for productivity, or for those fed up with the hassles of the city or the banality of the suburbs. Imagine holding a conference on a wide shady screened porch on the edge of the forest! It's completely possible. The recording industry has been using such locations for many years now, from upstate New York to the foothills of the Rockies.

"Where the deer and the antelope play, where seldom is heard a discouraging word and the skies are not cloudy all day..." [40]

Another typical wilderness office is the forest ranger's lookout or the scientist's base camp. The ranger's tiny space perched high above the trees is totally permeated by the atmosphere of natural world below. The base camps may be various typed of huts — wooden, metal or fiberglass structures, or they may be mobile trailer units. For the truly rugged people who want the full experience, small tents are the only way to go. Though the new stressed-skin types come in a great variety of colors and shapes and are relatively stable in windy storms, the older pole and guy wire type comes in sizes of more comfortable proportion, big enough for a cot, table and chair. One might work with great inspiration sitting in a director's chair by the camp fire. And then of course one could see the stars very well too, if the sky is clear.[41]

The temporary, yet rather stationery type of office for the individual or small group is very different than for the large organization. John Brinkerhoff Jackson describes with great perception how the military HQ in wartime revealed very direct and primitive methods of place-dominating and place-making raised to a vital emotional level of general involvement not experienced since the Dark Ages.[42] Examples range from the heraldry and regalia of the generals and their staff, to the Yankee spirit of a muddy sign over a foxhole on the line, "Last Chance for Gas". Back in the villages, the graffiti documented that "Kilroy was here". Spray paint battalions of urban youth gangs claim their turf in similar ways today. War seems to intensify every ritual behavior with a concentration of energy, perhaps spillover from the sustained adredalin-high maintained in states of threat and conflict.

"I'm on the road again,..."[43]

Truly mobile offices today are found in planes, boats, cars, trucks, buses, vans, pushcarts and perhaps even on the back or in the pocket.

The briefcase is the epitome of the portable office — boiled down to absolute essentials with pocket calculators and tape recorders. Futurists predict briefcases may someday accommodate total information systems complete with keyboard, video display and telecommunications. Vehicular offices have a wide range of possible accessories especially for communication/information storage and processing. Imagine an office sailing around the islands of the Aegean Sea with the company logo on the spinnaker! The office in a Lear Jet is the most typical fantasy of all. So why not make an earthbound place with the same sense of excitement? In the future we will be seeing offices orbiting in space, and as outposts on other planets.

PLACE:

LOCATION		SIZE		
CLASS	TYPE	100 - 5000 SF	5000 - 20,000 SF	20,000 - 800,000 SF
Urban: Downtown	Boulevard Park Square Plaza Corner Street End Side Street	room or suite off corridor	full floor to several floors	many floors to whole building
Transition	Warehouse Street Alley Piers and Wharfs Bridges	same	same	same
Neighborhood	Main Shopping Street Residential Street	storefront study house	showroom	NA
Small Town	Main Street Residential Street	same	same	same
Suburban/Exurban	Roadside @Hwy interchange @Activity corridors	room or suite	floor or whole building	one to several buildings
	Office Park	same	same	same
	Commerical Strip	storefront	showroom	NA
	Residential Street	study	NA	NA
Rural/Mobile	Fixed (Cabin, Lodge) Temporary (Tent, Hut) Mobile (Vehicles, Bags)			

The principle factors of office location, size, form and image affect each other in several ways. Size limits form and influences image, while location limits size and form. Form and image are interdependent reflections of location and organization. Once a basic location for an office building has been selected, the primary problems of building form, siting, parking and entry must be resolved simultaneously. Depending on the constraints of the site, program and budget, any one of these problems can limit the choices available. The greatest range of choices and, therefore, problems may be found in the suburban/exurban locations.

Since most exurban offices are inconvenient to public transportation, large parking areas are needed for employees' cars, as well as parking for visitors. It seems paradoxical to come to the country to look out across a sea of autos, but this is difficult to avoid. Hiding parking areas underneath or on top of the building is expensive and strongly influences the choice of structural bay dimension and building form. Grade level parking can be behind, in front or along the side of the building. Wherever possible, it is usually screened by bermed earth and trees. Practically every combination of these parking alternatives has been used.

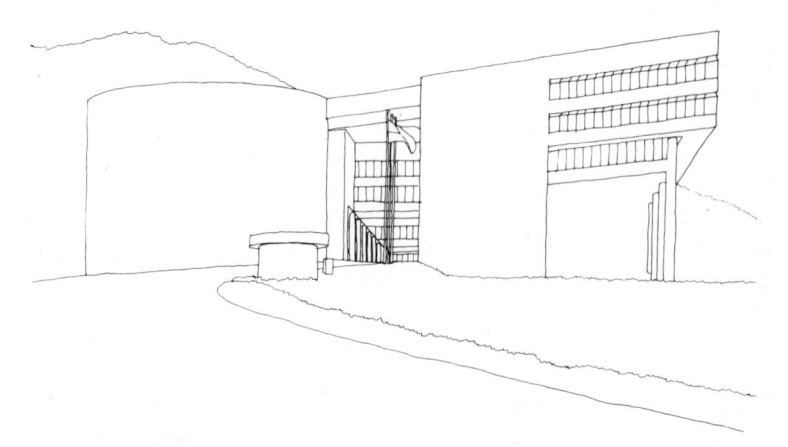

Desired degree of visual prominence, views, soil conditions and topography all influence the siting of the building. Sometimes the form of the building and parking requirements influence the exact siting, especially on small sites, but usually it is the other way around. Where the site is large, the building can be set far back from the road and screened by trees to create a low key corporate retreat. Or it can be placed at a corner of the site to preserve the natural landscape. Where a site has a change of grade, the building can sit on a ridge or hilltop for view and visual prominence, or just below the crest to maintain a low profile. Where buildings are set on a slope, parking is often terraced up and behind the structure. Sometimes the building is placed in the most difficult area so that the easier sites may be developed more economically in the future or sold. Other common features of site development include water formations such as streams and ponds, pedestrian trails, bike paths and general park areas. Large, formal structures tend to have informal landscaping, while smaller ones tend to have formal landscaping.

"Usually in such building types the ambiguity of automobile arrival most often leaves the whole question of the pedestrian arrrival sequence totally ignored..."[14]

The relationship of the access road, parking and building entry points can be difficult to resolve in the exurban office. Again, when the site is small, choices are limited. A short entry drive usually passes the main entry and continues on to the parking area. At larger sites, the entry drive may approach the front of the building formally, on axis, or wind romantically through the site and around the building. A very popular scheme allows glimpses of the building during the approach, finally revealing it at close range from a dramatic angle. Visitors parking is usually close to the main entrance, connected to it by landscaped or paved plazas. Where possible, employee parking is provided separately and connected to employee entrances by walks or bridges. Other common entry elements include flags, fountains and sculptures. In almost every case, the entry sequence is made as impressive as possible.

PLACE:
Form

"Thirty spokes share the wheel's hub;
It is the center hole that makes it useful.
Shape clay into a vessel;
It is the space within that makes it useful.
Cut doors and windows for a room;
It is the holes which make it useful.
Therefore profit comes from what is there;
Usefulness from what is not there." [45]

Form and space define each other, like black and white, or night and day. Forms, such as buildings, enclosures, cabinets, etc., define the space outside themselves at the same time that they define space inside. So when we talk about a form we should remember both the exterior and interior conditions.

Form/space making devices of the most basic kind are : the point (object or focus), the line (edge or boundary), the plane (enclosing membrane) and the volume (large masses of material). Each class of devices blends into the next one. Many points or objects set closely together create a line or boundary condition like stepping stones. A row of columns at the edge of a courtyard can create the effect of an enclosing plane. Many rows of bedsheets hanging in the sun to dry, can seem to be a volume, like a big marshmallow.

Different objects can play the role of these various elements, depending on the size or scale of the form/space involved. For example, a plane (overhead-horizontal type) can be a backlit panel of colorful fabric for a small group of people, or it can be a five foot deep by 200 foot square space frame canopy over an outdoor concert seating area. The most common type of overhead plane that makes a space for one person is the umbrella.

The basic distinctions between the possible devices in each of the groups: point, line, plane and volume, are determined by the physical location of the device relative to the form/space that it is making. A horizontal plane can be overhead, as we have already mentioned, or it can be a base platform (floor), an elevated platform (landing or balcony) or even a depressed platform (pit). **Architecture: Form, Space and Order** by Francis

D.K. Ching gives the most thorough and uncomplicated presentation of this basic vocabulary of form/space makers. His discussion of "Vertical Linear Elements" is a case in point.

"A vertical linear element, such as a column, establishes a point on the ground plane and makes it visible in space. Standing alone, a column is non-directional except for the path that would lead to it. Any number of axes can be made to pass through it. "When located within a defined volume of space, a column will articulate the space around it and interact with the enclosure of the space. A column can attach itself to a wall and articulate its surface. It can reinforce the corner of a space and de-emphasize the meeting of its wall planes. Standing within a space, a column can define zones of space within a room. "When centered within a room, a column will assert itself as the center of the space and define equal zones of space between itself and the surrounding wall planes. When offset, the column will define hierarchical zones of space that are differentiated by size, form and location."[46]

From screen walls and shadow lines to boulders and mountains, these basic elements and their variations can make all of the possible forms/spaces from the scale of single rooms to whole buildings to large complexes. As atoms come together to make molecules, so these elements combine into basic units which we can define as shapes and solids. Shapes include: circles, triangles, squares, hexagons, parallelograms, on down the list to the mobius strip, which is the bridge between two dimensional and three dimensional events. Each different shape has a different tradition of meanings or feelings associated with it. For example, in western civilization, the circle may represent the eternal or universal while the square may signify the rational. The five basic types of solids are known as the Platonic solids. Ching sets this group to include the sphere, cylinder, cone, pyramid and the cube. Others have described slightly different sets.[47]

Combinations and transformations of the platonic or regular solids can produce an infinite variety of irregular solids, with a corresponding blend of the related associations and values. These primary and secondary, regular and irregular shapes and solids may then be changed or further differentiated by the many processes of transformation. Processes most common in altering forms/spaces include multiplying the basic unit, subtracting one shape from another, or overlapping the patterns of units. The processes of dimensional change include twisting, bending, stretching, compressing and notching the form, just like it was a hunk of play dough.

"Forms translate into space certain movements of the mind." [48]

The origins and functions of the forms of office buildings become an increasing paradox. Methods of composition can be based on complexity and contradiction, or simplicity and rationality. Stravinsky, a famous modern composer, has written about the methods of composition in a way which might also apply to the generation of office forms:
"Music thus gains strength in the measure that it does not succumb to the seductions of variety. What it loses in questionable riches it gains in true solidity."
"Strength, says Leonardo da Vinci, is born of constraint and dies of freedom...Insubordination boasts of the opposite and does away with constraint in the ever disappointed hope of finding in freedom the principle of strength."
"A mode of composition that does not assign itself limits becomes pure fantasy." "So the danger lies not in the borrowing of cliche's. The danger lies in fabricating them and in bestowing on them the force of law, a tyranny that is merely a manifestation of romanticism grown decrepit."
"What is important for the lucid ordering of the work — for its crystallization — is that all the Dionysian elements which set the imagination of the artist in motion and make the lifesap rise must be properly subjugated before they intoxicate us and must finally be made to submit to the law: Apollo demands it."[49]

In addition to the factors of budget and site, the principle limits or guidelines for the development of the office form are the characteristics of the organization. Form should at least be a strong expression of the organization, but it may also go beyond this in some logical way to expand the notion of what the particular office is all about. If no two businesses are exactly the same, why should any two offices be the same? Of course, we need some similarities between buildings to maintain a sense of order and continuity in the environment. But each business requires something distinctive about its facilities as an asset for general marketing purposes. Conveniently, most architects would like to produce such distinctive facilities because that is the fun (if not the profit) of their profession.

"All forms are similar, yet none are the same, so that their chorus points the way to a hidden law."[50]

Architectural form as an issue involves more than just the overall shape of a building. There are three parts of any shape which are each as important in their own right, as the shape to which they belong.

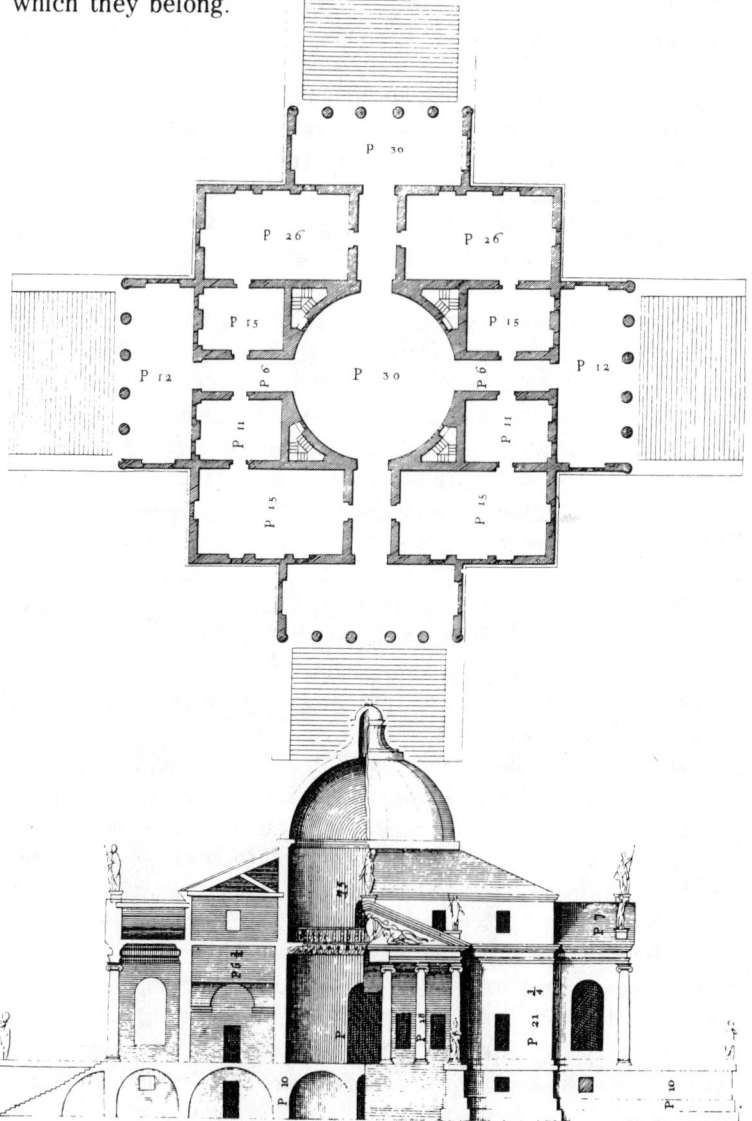

How does the building meet the sky? Does it have a head or crown? How does the building meet the street? Does it stand on feet and legs or sit on a wide cushion? How does it turn the corner? Does it give any signals before it makes the turn? The top, base and corners must be connected by the meat, bones and skin of the building. Whether or not the surface reveals the structure within seems to be more a question of image, since most types of forms can be developed as either skin or bones in final appearance.

The most general issue of architectural form is surprisingly the one to which the layman is most naturally sensitive. In its parts, as well as in their total effect, the form may feel one of two ways: balanced, stable and crystallized; or unbalanced, dynamic and in a constant state of change. These perceptions can be relatively subjective, but it is usually as much a visceral as a visual/intellectual response.

The final impression of architectural form is also perceived by most people on a gut level. The question of scale is the question of whether or not the form/spaces of a building are an appropriate size in proportion to the occupants. When one enters a space he can usually tell if it was built for him or a "chorus of Mack trucks".[51] "Man is the measure of all things."[52] This issue received great attention during the Renaissance, not only because of the general emphasis on man as the center of the universe, but also because of the invention of perspective drawing, an essential tool for understanding and manipulating relationships of scale. Some designers and theorists of the period went so far as to suggest that through the relation of a place to the human figural proportions, one might reconcile the classic dichotomy between body and mind.[53]

"During the middle of the 1960's, the countrified corporation became a commonplace feature of the American way of life, as big businesses, leaving the cities, scrammed to the suburbs, or sometimes further, to the sticks. The architectural results of this solemn migration have been too often a savaging of the terrain with if-you've-got-it, flaunt-it forms..."[54]

The choice of basic forms and subsequent refinements are influenced by several major factors. Actually, the forms of most offices are fairly simple, though they can be very impressive in size. This basic simplicity is necessitated by structural economics and standard office operations. The simplest and most economic structure is formed by square bays (column spacing) of moderate span. Standard office operations usually require a certain percentage of individual office areas, either fully partitioned or created with office landscaping elements.

Typical station modules are 10 by 10 or 10 by 15 feet, and so on in proportion at increments of 5 feet up to 30 feet, where a different set of guidelines comes into play. Therefore, a 20 by 20 or 30 by 30 bay structure is typical in office buildings. Less common is a 25 by 25 bay. Another factor of building economics which influences form is the fact that increasing the perimeter of the building increases the amount of skin materials required, and therefore increases the cost. The most economical form should be a square building. However, large square floors have more area that is farther away from the windows, natural light and view — i.e. less desirable space, than rectangular buildings with the same floor area and more perimeter. Skylighted, interior light wells and atriums cut down through the floors of the building to bring natural light and visual relief to the large space.

Many large offices require that a high percentage of the floor area be perimeter office space. For speculative buildings, this factor has a great influence on the marketability of the space. For non-speculative buildings, this factor is a response to the high percentage of executive personnel who need the prestige and privacy of a perimeter office. A variation of this factor is the requirement for a high percentage of corner office space, which is even more difficult to provide in an economical structure.[55]

The degree of operational independence in the departments of a corporate organization also affects the form. Highly independent, segmented operations permit a more spread out form, such as the linear blocks, linked pavilions or even the tower. Since these forms can create very long travel distances from end to end, they are inefficiant for offices with highly interdependent operations, which require more compact forms such as the cruciform or box with light court and other generally stout forms.

Site size and views help set the limits on the ultimate dimensions of the buildings and its orientation. Smaller sites pose strong limitations on form, usually generating compact, rectangular buildings. Site size permitting, form is influenced by desirable views and solar positions. Good views all around may suggest a cruciform building whereas good views to one side may suggest a linear approach.

The skyscraper is an architectural form that was originally developed to serve the needs of the office: large open floor areas with good light and ventilation in the center of the city.

The timely invention of the structural steel frame and the elevator just after the Civil War combined with the great demand for construction in Chicago after the devastating fire of 1871 and the energy of many young, talented and ambitious men to produce the first true skyscrapers and to develop a whole new architectural style for them.[56]

Tall buildings dominate every city today, except for those with special constraints. Construction of high rise office buildings in already congested downtown centers may create chaos in the surrounding streets for many months, but also provides an exciting show. The sidewalk superintendants of summer lunch hours maintain constant curiousity in the tedious progression, as billions of pieces of all kinds of stuff climb into the sky. When they are finished, these places are often the talk of the town, a strange mixture of boosterism and one-upmanship on many levels.

The prime economic incentives for skyscrapers usually require the maximum size allowed by code regulations.

The income return per rental square foot after mortgage, and financing expenses can be greatly enhanced in the project area range beyond a threshold level determined by the foundation expenses and other special equipment expenses. The greater the demand for space, the safer the risk for making money by building larger. This is a very simple idea and yet an ever changing condition, elusive in the complexity of compounded economic factors. The growth of the urban core is well beyond the control, if not the influence, of the urban planners.

In their place today we have image-makers and cheerleaders, who can create surges of real estate and construction activity by the blessings they bestow on the chosen neighborhoods.[57] All of the competitors must of course follow suit or be left behind. Some people call it the riskiest game in town, but it is also addictively exciting. The scale of the game in terms of direct economic payoffs may be modest by today's standards, relative to technical financial risks, but this is one game in business that has a real live game board with pieces that can be seen, touched and moved.

Such pleasures are just a frill compared to the ultimate challenge of coordinating all of the resources, interests and activities necessary to execute a large building project. Developers' dreams are saturated with a pure desire to meet this challenge. With all of the positive economic side effects of construction activity, it would seem only natural that the Federal government would reinforce the growth trends at almost no actual expense by providing partial loan guarantees, at least for interim, if not long term financing. This could reduce both performance bond and financing interest expense and increase the scope of potential projects. Inflation rates, tax rates and even unemployment rates might all be changed for the better.

At the same time that demand for office space has grown, so has the realization that unique, distinctive quality architecture may bring premium rentals and rock bottom vacancy rates. Whatever it takes to go for the top of the market is usually worth it, especially when the top demands the latest benefits and/or accessories, like dining and athletic clubs, or bicycle parking decks. A heliport is another image and rent boosting feature. But the best feature of all is still a knock-out design.

As a result of all these interrelated forces, the forms of big office buildings have been undergoing a little organizing response. After decades of refined, restrained boxes holding their skirts up around their ankles, we are witnessing all kinds of variations on the standard theme. These follow the basic issues already discussed: top, base, corner and skin. Tops are wearing all different kinds of hats. Bases engulf plazas and atriums. Corners are built out, sheared away or eroded. And the display of colored glass in some of the curtain walls could make a peacock blush. Last but not least, the basic forms also seek new variety, despite continuing site constraints. The square and rectangular plans of the basic tower and slab are becoming triangles and quarter circles raised in extrusion, or pyramids or truncated cylinders. We even have seen a few trapezoids and parallelapipeds slinking around.[58] Once the atrium craze "rediscovered" the principles of light wells (first used in the days of structural limitation) as useful in the current days of energy crisis, the hypnotic spell of the glass box was cracked, opening the Pandora's Box inside.

For the suburban and exurban offices, three basic form options for high percentage perimeters are: linear pavilion; cruciform; and box with non-enclosed light courts. Many form variation are possible by combining these three approaches, and other transformations of form. There are two basic variations in the vertical dimension. The building can step up and out to provide shading and possible energy savings. Or it can step down and out to create roof terraces.

When the programmed building area becomes very large, another set of form options comes into play. Boxes along circulation spines and linked pavilions are popular schemes well suited for decentralized departmental operations in situations where visual building mass needs to be minimized. A formalized variation is the infill grid organization which creates closely spaced and/or linked buildings with plazas, courts or light wells in the grid spaces left open.

The second major option is the campus form of separated buildings spread out over the site, which is very popular for large speculative developments. Usually the units vary from one to the next in form and/or materials to prevent visual monotony and create identity for each location in the development. The third option, building up rather than out, is available where height restrictions permit, most often in the office parks near major roadways and away from residential developments. These taller buildings show the urban form types of tower and slab and their variants. Such buildings seem to be "suburban waiting to become urban" as city sprawl fills in around them.[59]

Sometimes, exurban offices are close to the roadway and by design try to maximize impact on passing motorists with large signs, graphics, architectural devices and extravagant landscaping. Buildings set far back from the road and hidden by trees resemble those built on isolated sites. A most architecturally interesting office building along the road presents a zig-zag mirrored wall. Passing motorists, see fractured reflections of themselves in the surrounding landscape. The resulting effect like a kinetic billboard, heightens the motorist's sense of speed. Another type of roadside building which seems to actively involve itself with the experience of passing motorists points a corner towards the road, instead of being parallel to it. Such buildings seem to move, to turn around, as one passes by.

Medium rise is the traditional size of European cities and the halls of government in Washington D.C. The benefits of the atrium are very noticeable in this project class, which may also exhibit rare geometries, curving planes or

palazzo "pizzazz". [60]

Another popular ploy is the "pile of boxes", a form that generates a unity in plurality. The original stock of medium rise buildings, the old warehouse blocks, remain unchanged in basic form. The high ceilings, heavy timber or concrete frames, wooden floors and plain brick walls are principal assets. The inefficient industrial sash can be replaced with insulating windows, and new connections between floors can be created when the structure is rehabilitated for office or commercial loft use. Such economies may leave room in the budget for the architect to play some special games in order to enhance the image and other marketable assets. The large open floor areas, usually 25 to 50 feet wide and 50 to 200 feet long, are ideally suited to natural office modules.

The same thing may be said of the vintage Victorian townhouse. Plain or fancy, brick or brownstone, from the proper rows of Baltimore to the painted ladies of San Francisco, these darlings are treasured as both residential and office space. In addition to the high ceilings and wood floors of the warehouses, the townhouses also feature fireplaces, bay windows, and elaborate wood detailing for added warmth and elegance. The general townhouse features of yards and small porches are the low rise equivalent of a penthouse office terrace and very chic. The courtyards of New Orleans are the creme de la creme. Standard party wall construction, i.e. a wall shared between two structures, affords tremendous opportunities for the elegance and excitement of the building skin draped up the front, over the top and down the back. On the other end of the design spectrum, shell games can be played by carving out new spaces or constructing elaborate rotated mazes within the simple walls.

The less common office locations, in store fronts and show rooms provide similar potential with new twists. The storefront window puts everything on a stage, so the interior space may be elaborated as a mythical setting, using divider/storage walls as the "scenery", accented by theatrical lighting. The long, wide and high showroom space of auto dealerships, furniture outlets and groceries, may be capitalized with plant-filled, free-standing, metal jungle gym mezzanines under glowing skylights.

We are already generally familiar with the exterior and interior forms of detached dwellings converted to office use. Special conditions can arise if the building is listed with the National Register of Historic Places. Although a developer can receive tax credits up to 25 per cent of the renovation costs, alteration of the building envelope can be restricted. Another hassle with making offices out of homes on the edges of small downtowns is dealing with zoning restrictions, parking requirements in particular.[61]

The form of interior spaces and rooms may compliment the shell and structure, and try to capitalize on its special features.

Unusual forms usually generate unusual rooms. Conversely, surprising events may hide behind an unassuming facade. The forms of office interiors and rooms in terms of organization, people and things have already been discussed. Such organizations may be clustered, linear or radial. They can be patterned as a reflection of the city environment itself. Shifting layers of walls, space and light can be used to achieve the proper atmosphere. The whole thing can be as carefully crafted as a fine piece of furniture with brass reveals and wood moulding trims.

However, the basic principle of interior form, from the traditional salon to the open office, is the balanced proportion of length to width to height. The golden rules of Pythagoras, Palsidio and others help to avoid spaces which feel like bowling alleys or chimney stacks, and help the occupant feel centered in the space.[62]

"You have noticed that everything an Indian does is in a circle, and that is because the Power of the world always works in circles, and everything tries to be round...Even the seasons form a great circle in their changing, and always come back again to where they were. The life of man is a circle from childhood to childhood and so it is in everything where Power moves. Our teepees were round like the nests of birds and these were set in a circle, the nations hoop, a nest of many nests where the Great Spirit meant for us to hatch our children."[63]

PLACE:
Image

There is no one true image for an office, except perhaps the image of success. In the corporate world, success seems most easily understood as a static statement like, "We have come through the woods and now we're on top," rather than a statement reflecting the real process of business and office work in general, like "We are on a road towards many goals, and although we make good progress every day, the horizon is always out there calling..." The image of the office is how we see ourselves, as well as how others see us. Many times the most important aspect of an image is what we take for granted.

The image of an office, because of the primary factors of organization, location and form will naturally reveal the essence of the business within that office. Care is needed, however, since response to the primary factors may be inappropriate, resulting in an image that might say things about a corporation that in fact are not true. The vast industry of marketing and public relations is based on the critical importance of images and the information they convey.

It seems wise for any successful business person who wants to stay that way, to learn what office buildings can say about the values of the business inside. For example, a business with a very fine office may appear to have a lot of money. That may or may not be true. What is true is that the office in question has clearly demonstrated that they have spent money, or invested it. If one looks carefully at how the office is developed as an asset: a piece of real estate, collection of furniture and equipment, a conspicuous display and a sincere effort to promote the well-being and productivity of the work force, then one would be in a position to understand the basic nature or motivating principles of the business in question. Whether it is a client, a competitor or one's own organization, the more we know about it, the better our chances for achieving and maintaining that state of success.

Despite the extreme differences of image-making opportunities between the high-rise urban office building, medium-rise or low-rise exurban office building, and even a very small structure in either an urban or rural setting, some primary image types are available to them all. The basic image of an office can be either people-oriented, i.e. humanistic, or the image can be machine-oriented, i.e. technological. The first type might seem to carry the impression of a "temple of capitalism" or "corporate domicile", while the second type might suggest the concept of a "business machine" or "corporate laboratory".

"Business Machines and Corporate Laboratories"

Office buildings constructed and clad in metal have direct associations with machines. The architectural tradition of the Machine Asesthetic contributes to the associations of this image: technological, efficient, modern, disciplined and formal. When used for an office building, this image type can connote high class and prestige in the vision of a classic Miesien steel frame. The metal skin/strip window building seems more sleek, steamlined and contemporary than the frame type.

Many metal buildings resemble warehouses which can have both negative (cheap) and postive (cheap chic/high tech) associations, depending on the quality of the design, not the actual cost of the materials. Many people experience metal buildings as being cold, unfriendly and inhuman places, compared to masonry buildings. But business can often be cold, unfriendly and even ruthless. As office buildings go, however, "there are times when the basic black dress or the well-tailored suit is not only appropriate, but welcome."[64]

The color of the metal in combination with the type of glass used modifies the images of these business machine buildings. Black means serious business while white may suggest honest business. Shiny aluminum can connote a very contemporary, slick, fast-paced operation. The most popular metal office building formula is the corten steel type. The metal surface develops a self-protecting thin coat of rust by oxidation, which gives it the distinctive reddish-brown color. This material was first used in an architectural application in 1964. It creates an especially pleasing image on heavily wooded sites.

"Temples to Capitalism"

Many concrete office buildings fall into this category because of associations with stone construction. Stone once was used only for important structures such as temples and civic edifices because it was strong and durable connoting stability, as well as costly, connoting prestige. Since concrete is usually experienced as a warmer material than steel, concrete buildings can have a warmer or more humanistic image. But concrete is also heavier than steel and so concrete buildings can seem very imposing, massive and even oppresive compared to steel buildings. Concrete buildings which express the structural frame seem very traditional due to similarities with classical stone architecture. The choice of glass refines the sense of formality, openess and style. For concrete buildings with strip windows the levitation of concrete over glass can create a perplexing visual impression and perhaps suggest that the corporation inside also has unique abilities.

"Corporate Domiciles"

Some office buildings today bypass the standard images described above in favor of a more residential look. This may be done in order to blend with the surrounding environment, to reflect the type of business carried out, or simply by necessity, as in the case of very small offices. The kinds of house images employed include the cottage, as in "cottage industry", manor, mansion, chateau, palace and castle. Manors, mansions and chateaus are very popular in second rate design office parks and speculative buildings. They exhibit the full range of tacky historical styles found in the surrounding suburban housing developments: colonial, ante-bellum, georgian, french provincial, etc. Palace and castle images are achieved in better designs through the use of materials, inflections of massing, entry treatments and landscaping. A recently proposed headquarters design created a palace image with a symmetrical scheme of bent linear pavilions on either side of a domed, light-welled block. The residential reference is underscored with a tongue-in-cheek, but also economical and innovative use of aluminum clapboard siding for the exterior wall cladding.

Office buildings which look like houses may seem more friendly and approachable than other offices. They also reflect the fact that many people spend more of their waking hours at the office than at home. The office becomes the home-away-from-home. Corporate domiciles show a major step in the evolution of the office building type as it adapts to the non-urban environment. As discussed previously in the sections on locations and form, the original case of the office/house is the actual house structure which has been renovated for office use. All of the standard options for upgrading the image of a house are available for upgrading the office/house including color and texture of surface materials, awnings, exterior light fixtures, dormers, etc.

"The shape of an office building in cities is often the product of a predetermining push and pull of forces caused by maximizing the use of super-expensive land and the limitations of local zoning restrictions...a reduction of such confining pressures in the suburbs has allowed a much wider variety of design solutions to suit the unique circumstances of individual neighborhoods, environments and users. If consistent characteristics are to be found, they will occur in the need to provide more employee amenities, such as places to eat, park, shop and relax, and in the ability to appear less overpowering and assertive than their urban counterparts — while reflecting a desired prestige to their owners."[65]

The aggregate image of the building in relation to the site can be internally consistent or contradictory. Buildings which try to blend in or stand out and fail, create an ineffectual and sometimes comical image, while those which succeed can create the images described below.

A highly formal building with formal siting and landscaping can create a stiff image of proper, button down decorum: a strong organization that firmly controls the physical, and by suggestion, the economic environment of its operation: the corporation as conqueror. If the building is large, the effect can be overbearing. A formal building with more informal siting and landscaping can create the traditionally Oriental image of a well organized, sensitive firm in counterpoint or balance with an environment it neither can nor wishes to conquer or imitate: a firm which probably listens very well. A more informal building with formal siting and landscaping can create the curious image of an organization which calls attention to itself by emphasizing its surroundings and avoiding pretentiousness. Or maybe such firms want others to think more of them than they do of themselves. And finally, the informal building with informal siting and landscaping, can create a casual, relaxed image of the corporation blending into the environment, a capitalization on the back-to-nature trend.

A particularly important aspect of the overall office image is the treatment of the entrance area. Though many plaza accessories are available, from flags and fountains to benches and planters, care must be taken that these are integrated into the overall image and not just tacked on like so much gaudy jewelry. These elements may be used sparingly for an image of grandeur and austere spaciousness, or they can be combined in dense, closely spaced arrangements for an effect of heightened intrigue and romance. Of all the parts of an office, the entry is perhaps the most important area to develop with a free and generous hand. Besides impressing visitors, a beautiful and exciting entry can ensure that everyone begins the work day with a positive attitude.

Offices in the city generally cover most, if not all, of the possible site area. However, zoning setback regulations can allow builders to construct taller buildings in return for giving back some of the site area to the street space in the form of plazas, arcades and atruims. Though some lobbies may have more security personnel than others, these spaces generally seem to be very public. Because of the density of buildings in the city, urban office structures themselves seem to have the basic sense of being a public place, best illustrated by the swarms of people continuously flowing in and out of the elevator banks.

In contrast to this, the nature of public and private space in the more isolated suburban and exurban offices is very different. As in the surrounding residences, these smaller, freestanding office buildings occupy property whose legal boundaries are rarely prominently marked, except perhaps by the end of the parking lot. Though the asphalt, lawns, plazas, woodlands or landscaped areas surrounding each of these offices may seem to be as openly accessible as public parkland, they are still felt to be the private territory of the residents and visitors to the particular building on the lot. The understanding of these boundaries is based on the American culture and custom that one's domain extends beyond the walls of the dwelling to encompass a sheltering belt of space to keep one safe and separated from the dangerous world outside. Daniel Boone has made perhaps the most memorable remarks on "elbow room". This sensitivity to territory is illustrated by the fact that when corporations do invite general public use of their estates, it is only in specially designated areas.

It has been suggested by some landscape analysts that exurban offices intentionally attempt to become a public visual amenity, but this is probably only the unintentional by-product of the primary desire to project a good image for the company. Homes for corporations are no more public amenities than homes for people, which try to project a good image for the family. And if the general public did perceive the transplanted offices as amenities, then why do surrounding residential communities demand that the interlopers be as low profile and "invisible" as possible? I'm sure everyone enjoys seeing a fine building along the road as one passes safely by in a car, but there is something threatening about seeing an office building rising out of the trees behind the patio. The motives for the original suburban exodus are too ingrained for most people to tolerate visual reminders of the city too close to home.

"I can't talk about my singing; I'm inside it. How can you describe something you're inside of?" [66]

As an expression of the many activities and organizations inside, an office building cannot succeed unless its image somehow relates contents to surrounding context. This connection is by no means an easy thing to accomplish. Designers can use very sophisticated language in their analysis of how a design might integrate building with environment. Most people can sense in a very direct and basic way whether or not a building fits in. Carrying on existing patterns of size, shape and surface treatment is a simple method, but can also often lead to unnecessary conformity and monotony.

The real secret to creating an office image with contextual connections is to look beyond the surface of things for the underlying themes and motifs which give any particular place it unique character. A fishing village is very different from a mining town. Every place has some special qualities which form the essence of the personality of that place, from Dallas to Terre Haute. Our world is blessed with a fascinating diversity of human environments, which is one reason why tourism is such a big business. In order to be most successful, the image of the office building must reflect and reinforce these particular aspects of local culture and tradition.

One very obvious tradition which differs from place to place is that of architectural ornamentation. As in the case of ritual, we tend to think of ornaments as suitable only for special occasions, and not as a part of daily life.

The Puritan heritage of our founding fathers in America cast a dim view towards ornamentation as a sinful display of egotism and pride. But the sensitively crafted details incorporated into many of the older buildings around us seem more to communicate a message of joy, caring and even love. The human spirit can soar to similar heights in the creation and appreciation of a poem cast in iron as it does for a song wrought with pen and paper.

"...architecture, like any other cultural product...is a system... accumulating layers of meaning and sense, and constituting one of the many symbolic spheres instituted by society...symbols... read as a 'text'...supporting ideas or concepts beyond describing the particular function of the place..."[67]

Though it isn't always necessary to understand the words of a song in order to enjoy the tune, one can unusually get more satisfaction when the message or meaning of the music is known. In the days before newspapers and television, when society evolved in a slow, gradual way, almost everyone understood the meaning of even the most obscure ornaments on the local church. It was easy because there wasn't much else to look at.

Today there are so many concepts and values competing for "air time", so many events and objects challenging each other for our attention, that is seems nearly impossible to hope for a modern system of architectural ornamental expression that would be easily understood by everyone. The Chicago architect, Louis Sullivan tried to develop such a system by combining cosmic geometry with the organic forms of plants and flowers. In his system for example, the curve and spiral symbolized life, stars symbolized transfigured souls and the circle on the square represented the cosmic heavens above the immutable earth and the cycles of life and being. The ornamental system of the Art Deco period in the 1930's received much wider exposure. The greatest Art Deco buildings were offices such as the Chrysler Building or the Empire State Building or Rockefeller Center. The strong hard edge geometries and activated designs conveyed the sense of the dynamic energy of the machine. Art Deco ornaments reflected the age in which society generally cast aside the fears about technology, to make the machine a romantic object in itself.

Many songs have claimed that you can't turn back the hands of time. Though we might love the beautiful old buildings of colonial days, or the humming dynamos of Art Deco, it is foolishness to

174 TRANSFORMING YOUR OFFICE

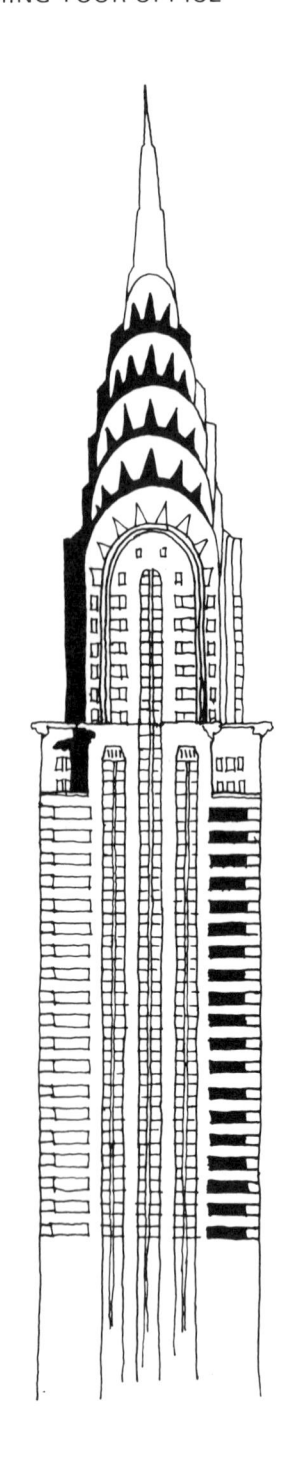

blindly recreate such buildings without also reflecting the ideas and values of the here and now.

Alvin Toffler has explained how the splintering of mass society into an increasing number of special groups and subcultures produces an ever increasing array of symbols and codes. If a designer wishes to enrich a building with ornamental details that might be commonly understood, he might find the solution to the communication problem through the use of the basic fantasy images which still populate our dreams. Heroes, romantic or villanous figures maintain an almost universal appeal in the form of the gypsy and the jetsetter, the cowboy and the spaceman, the islander and the mountaineer. It seems likely that a richer source for popular design elements might be found in the novels of Zane Grey or even in a Harlequin romance, rather than in the esoteric professional design journals. As long as the images derived reflect the deeper aspects of human nature, there should be no fears of banality or misunderstanding.

To incorporate such meaningful elements into the image of the office is a challenge which may be taken up by architects in the coming years. Then we may witness a complete renaissance of the office from the inside out.

"richness comes from layers of visual, verbal symbols with resonant meanings..." [68]

The motifs and figures of well-known myths and legends can enrich the image of the office as a place of struggle, energy, action and growth. Of course, the various metaphors of the maverick entrepeneur, from the swashbuckling pirate to the gold prospector, should not be mere cartoons pasted onto the surface of the building. To quote a myth or legend without adding a new angle to it, or without showing a connection to its evolution, in other words, to treat the myth or legend like it just popped out of thin air, will create a shallow image that seems unreal and fake. The viewer would look at the carving or casting or whatever and think "Gee, that's a cowboy on horseback chasing down a stampeding steer. Those rip-roarin' wild west days sure were somethin'." Unfortunately, the viewer has not been stimulated to draw the connection between the image and his own personal situation.

In order to "demythify" the myths so that they allow new associations in the viewer's mind and therefore can generate new meanings, the details of the image of the myth or legend must be transformed.[69]

For example, the cowboy could still be riding the horse in pursuit of a steer, except he could be wearing a three piece suit instead of chaps. Or perhaps the steer's hide could be made of money. The goal of such twisted images is to convey the original basic myth and then hold the viewer's interest with the intriguing possibilities of additional meanings. The richer the image, the greater the number of potential interpretations. "The effect of aesthetic perception can reorient the perceivers' sense of reality."[70]

The famous visions of fantasy environments created by such artists as M. C. Escher, Hieronymous Bosch, Bertoia, Piranesi, Raphael, Max Ernst and Salvidor Dali demonstrate the dream as a vehicle of entertainment and inspiration.[71] The image of an office could definitely benefit from the meaningful visual enrichment of the typically boring minimal appearance which has dominated the image of the office since the 1950's.

"...subversion must produce its own chiaroscura..."[72]

"...work which aims at penetrating the solidity of blindly conventional constructions aims at unfolding the imaginary symbolic universe that architecture proposes and represses, to show that architecture as an opaque apparition (or black hole) against a background of transparent myths..."[73]

The primary components of an office image include its basic spatial features and the nature of the enclosure. We physically experience the size and shape of rooms, views to the outside or adjoining interior areas and the general sequence of volumes animated by lights, sounds and spatial focus. The way the body reacts to these physical sensations sends messages to the brain which are received as the feeling or meaning of the place. Whether the image is open and inviting, twisted and confusing, heavy and protecting, or light and airy depends on the fundamental haptic properties of the place.[74] Each person develops a natural understanding of this aspect of image through repeated experience of real places. The seemingly universal standard by which such image qualities are judged may even be rooted in the shared genetic heritage of human beings as an animal species, whose very survival once depended in part on the ability to determine the safeness of a refuge according to its image.

With all of the themes and pieces taken together as a whole, the image of the office expresses the philosophy or world view which is the foundation of the organization. The firm's operations and goals are developed through its perceptions and interpretations of the relations between people and things, power and order, being and time, etc.

If, as many great thinkers have suggested, the ability to comprehend this world depends on a belief in some sort of cosmic order, then the image of the office must also reflect that sense of order. But on the other hand, if the reality of that underlying order is the flux and flow of unpredictable events and changing physical circumstances, then the image of the office should temper its expression of order accordingly. The first chapter of this book was devoted to the balance between rational and irrational or planned and unplanned actions which are both necessary and inevitable in successful office operations.

The beauty and strength of the traditional modern architectural style becomes poignantly human when it is no longer executed with absolute machine-like precision. The odd conditions, the twists and kinks where the general order of the image stands on its head, will enable the office to remind its users and inhabitants that the emotional and irrational functions are a vital component of successful office life for the individual as much as for the total organization.

— PLACE 179

"Man's understanding
of being
is his openess
to being."[75]

"...Chaos is very near...its nearness, yet it avoidance, gives force..."

                Robert Venturi

"...Disorder is the order which we cannot see..."

                Henri Bergson

"We do not associate the idea of dream with out strenuous hours of thought and deed in the selfsame broad daylight. Nor do we the stars at noon — but they are there. So is a dream there, within every human — day and night unceasingly."

              Louis Henri Sullivan

EPILOGUE:
Office, Culture and Society

"Societies produce parallel and interconnected systems of expression and statement which reflect a total complex of meaning and values...each component part of a society has a homologous relationship to every other part..."[1]

Office buildings, television programs, and interstate roadways all share the characteristics of being both a reflection of, and an influence on the national character. These influences direct the future of our society by defining its values and goals and by reinforcing the myths and symbols of desired behavior patterns.[2] Civilization grows in response to the combined forces of history and geography at the local, national and international levels.[3] Throughout the growth of civilization, man has pursued aesthetic pleasures for their own sake, as well as an effort to define the world and his place in it.

The ideas which man expresses in art become the units of cultural evolution.[4] Societies which have been called more primitive than our own often seem to have a much deeper understanding of the functions of artistic, cultural expression. Art is both the environment and the actions one performs in it, from the snow fields of the Eskimos to the dusty courtyards of the Pueblos.[5] Art is a celebration of the form itself as well as the ideas associated with it.

Sometimes the environment produced by a careless and inattentive society inadvertently becomes a powerful cultural art form, in response to the various pressures which control the development of that society. We can often see this in our cities and sometimes on the commercial strip. For example, the dialogue between the office towers that rise high above the urban crowd finds meaning in the ma or the space between obelisks and ishtars generate imaginary forcefields; "men on the chess board sit up and tell you where to go..."[6]

"It is culture that brings out the full value of taste and gives it a chance to prove its worth simply by its application. The artist imposes a culture upon himself and ends by imposing it upon others. That is how tradition becomes established. A real tradition is not the relic of a past that is irretrievably gone, it is a living force, that animates and informs the present..."[7]

Whether a person cares or not, he influences his environment as much as it influences him. These are times when the circle becomes almost deadly. As a statement of who we are, the environment has the power to change a person's identity, for better or worse as the case may be. Because of this general interdependence, the changing office environment will have a massive impact on the evolution of society and on the kind of people which office users and their children become. But this is a two-way street. Anyone who wishes to have a hand in shaping his own future, or the future of his culture, can learn about his working and living environment. The habitat must be understood and respected before people can guide it to meet their personal needs.

"...The enhancement of well being can be achieved through an environmental response to the psychic," as well as the physical "needs of the people."[8]

The sort of offices that are built reflect the values of our society as a whole. If we can learn to see what these buildings say about us, we might become more aware of the direction in which we head. Such insights might cause a total reevaluation of purpose by some firms, while others may open the throttle to full speed. In either case, the reduction of uncertainties and confusing tricks of fate puts the magic back at the service of the corporation. Office planning in the future must be a rich mixture of science, religion and art. It must be founded on moral, humanistic principles as much as on productive technologies and the goal of capital gains. Bon Voyage.

NOTES

ONE: PROCESS

1. Toffler, Alvin. **The Third Wave.** New York: Bantam, 1980.
2. Ibid.
3. Ibid., quotation of Randy Goldfield of Booz Allen and Hamilton.
4. Ibid., quotation of organizational theorist Tony Judge.
5. Ibid.
6. Ibid.
7. Ibid.
8. Schopenhauer, **The World Will and Idea.** translated by Haldane and Kemp. London: Kegan Paul, Trench, Trubner & Co., Ltd., 1907. Excerpt printed in **The Age of Idealogy.** Henry D. Aiken, New York: Mentor, 1956.
9. Christiansson, Carl. **The Office: How to Plan for Human Beings.** Stockholm: unpublished, 1977, quotation of author Goran Palm.
10. Studs Terkel. **Working.** New York: Avon, 1974.
11. Watts, Alan. **Does It Matter.**
12. Dass, Baba Ram. Journey of Awakening. New York: Bantam, 1978 quotation of Grudjeiff.
13. Jagger, Dean.
14. Probst, Robert. **The Office — an organization based on change.** Ann Arbor, Michigan: Herman Miller, 1969.
15. Carpenter, Edmund. **They Became What They Beheld.** New York: Ballantine, 1970 quotation Robbe-Grillet.
16. Op.Cit.
17. Stravinsky, Igor. **Poetics of Music: In the Form of Six Lessons.** Cambridge: Harvard University Press 1970.
18. Fuller, R. Buckminster. **Utopia or Oblivion.** New York: Bantam, 1969.
19. Singer, Jerome L. **Daydreaming.** New York: Random House, 1966.
20. Bloomer, Kent C. and Moore, Charles W. **Body, Memory, Architecture.** New Haven: Yale University Press 1977.
21. Johnson, Diane Chalmers. "Louis Sullivan and American Art Nouveau". **New Free Style, A. D. Design Profile.** Ian Latham, editor. London: Architectural Design, 1980.

22. Kubler, George. "Renascence and Disjunction in the Art of Mesoamerican Antiquity". **Ornament: VIA III, Journal of the Graduate School of Fine Arts, University of Pennsylvania.** Stephen Kieran editor, Philadelphia: Falcon Press, 1977. quotation of Henri Fogillon, La Vie des Formes. Paris: Alcan, 1939.
23. Johnson, Ibid., quotation of Louis Sullivan.
24. Tsu, Lao. **Tao Te Ching.** translated by Gia-Fu Feng and Jane English. New York: Random House, 1977, originally written in 6th century B.C.
25. Kozinski, Jerzy. **Being There.**
26. Reagan's Republicans.
27. Studs Terkel. Ibid., quotation of I Corinthians 3:13.
28. Jaynes, Julian. **The Origins of Consciousness in the Breakdown of the Bicameral Mind.** Princeton: Princeton University Press, 1976.
29. Focillon, Henri.
30. Singer, Jerome L. Ibid.
31. Bonta, Juan Pablo. conference presentation, "Critique of the Conference Proceedings". **Making Dreams Come True: Design in Aid of Fantasy.** San Francisco Center for Architecture and Urban Studies, February 7, 1981.
32. Piaget, Jean. **Origins of Intelligence in Children.** translated by Margaret Cook, New York: International University Press, 1952.
33. Bonta, Juan Pablo. Ibid.
34. Weick, Karl E. **Social Psychology of Organizing.** Reading, Mass.: Addison-Wesley, 1979.
35. Tavis, Alexander. "Concept Outline for Architectural Organization and Management: The Habitat Provision Process". unpublished course material. University of Illinois, Urbana, Illinois, 1977.
36. Probst, Robert. Ibid.
37. Ibid.
38. Williams, A. Richard. **The Urban Stage.** 1981.
39. Scully, Vincent J. **Louis I. Kahn.** New York: Braziller, 1962 quotation of Kahn.
40. Legorreta, Ricardo. conference presentation, "Designing for Tourists' Dreams". **Making Dreams Come True: Design in Aid of Fantasy.** San Francisco Center for Architecture and Urban Studies, February 7, 1981.
41. Woodbridge, Sally. "Fantasies of the California Home". **Making Dreams Come True: Design in Aid of Fantasy.** San Francisco Center for Architecture and Urban Studies, February 4, 1981.
42. Singer, Jerome L. Ibid.
43. Flippo, Chet. "Checking in with Joseph Heller". **Rolling Stone.** April 16, 1981. quotation of Joseph Heller.
44. **Rolling Stone.** interview quotation of Richard Dreyfuss.
45. Singer, Jerome L. Ibid.
46. Jaynes, Julian. Ibid., quotation of St. Augustine at Carthage.
47. Astor, Brooke. "Wisdom of Follies". **Architectural Digest.** May, 1981.
48. Singer, Jerome L., Ibid.
49. Ibid.
50. Ibid.
51. Ibid.
52. Ibid.
53. Riley, Robert. "The Landscape of Memory." unpublished manuscript. Urbana, Illinois, 1978.
54. Bonta, Juan Pablo. Ibid.
55. Riley, Robert. Ibid.
56. Ibid.
57. Singer, Jerome L. Ibid.

58. Singer, Jerome L. Ibid.
59. Ibid.
60. Ibid.
61. Ibid.
62. Ibid.
63. Ibid.
64. Ibid.
65. Ibid.
66. Ibid.
67. Ibid.
68. Ibid.
69. Ibid.
70. Ibid.
71. Ibid.
72. Ibid.
73. Ibid.
74. Ibid.
75. Fuller, R. Buckminster. Ibid.
76. Carpenter, Edmund. Ibid.
77. Fuller, R. Buckminster. Ibid.
78. Singer, Jerome L. Ibid.
79. Stravinsky, Igor. Ibid.
80. Ibid.
81. Ibid.
82. Clark, Sir Kenneth. **Leonardo da Vinci.** New York Penguin, 1959.
83. Stravinsky, Igor. Ibid.
84. Watts, Alan. Ibid.
85. Stravinsky, Igor. Ibid.
86. Hein, Piet.
87. Watts, Alan. Ibid.
88. Stavinsky, Igor. Ibid.
89. Jackson, John Brinkerhoff. conference presentation, "The Renaissance Dream of the House". **Making Dreams Come True: Design in Aid of Fantasy.** San Francisco Center for Architecture and Urban Studies. February 5, 1981.
90. Sagan, Carl. **Cosmos.** New York: Random House, 1980.
91. Rosenfeld, Edward. **The Book of Highs.** New York Quadrangle, 1973.
92. Stravinsky, Igor. Ibid.
93. Singer, Jerome L. Ibid.
94. Watts, Alan. Ibid.
95. Singer, Jerome L. Ibid.
96. Ibid.
97. Ibid.
98. Studs Terkel. Ibid.
99. Klee.
100. Singer, Jerome L. Ibid.

TWO: POWER

1. Studs Terkel. **Working.** New York: Avon, 1974, quotation of William Faulkner.
2. Something which I often try to remind myself.
3. Campbell, Glenn.
4. Tsu, Lao. **Tao Te Ching.** translated by Gia-Fu Feng and Jane English. New York: Random House, 1972. Originally written in 6th century B.C.
5. Singer, Jerome L. **Daydreaming.** New York: Random House, 1966.
6. Ibid.
7. Probst, Robert. **The Office — an organization based on change.** Ann Arbor, Michigan: Herman Miller, 1974.
8. Ibid.
9. Singer, Jerome L. Ibid.
10. Baldridge, Letitia. **Amy Vanderbilt's Complete Book of Etiquette: a guide to contemporary living.** Revised and expanded. Garden City, New York, Doubleday, 1978.
11. Jefferson Airplane.
12. Wallechinsky, David. **What Really Happened to the Class of 65?.**
13. Scully, Vincent J. **Louis I. Kahn.** New York: Braziller, 1962 quotation of Kahn.
14. Bloomer, Kent C. and Moore, Charles W. **Body, Memory, and Architecture.** New Haven: Yale University Press, 1977.
15. Ibid.
16. Fuller, R. Buckminster. **Utopia or Oblivion.** New York: Bantam, 1969.
17. Studs Terkel. Ibid.
18. Ibid.
19. Probst, Robert. Ibid.
20. Ibid.
21. Ibid.
22. Ibid.
23. The Beatles.
24. Christiansson, Carl. **The Office: How to Plan for Human Beings.** unpublished manuscript, Stockholm, Sweden, 1977.
25. Ouch, William. **Theory Z.** Reading, Mass. Addison-Wesley, 1981.
26. Woodbridge, Sally. conference presentation, "Fantasies of the California Home". **Making Dreams Come True: Design in Aid of Fantasy.** San Francisco Center for Architecture and Urban Studies, February 4, 1981.
27. "Endpaper". **Rolling Stone.** April 16, 1981.
28. Ching, Francis D. K. **Architecture: Form, Space & Order.** New York: Van Nostrand Reinhold Company, 1979.
29. Probst, Robert. Ibid.
30. Weick, Karl I. **Social Psychology of Organizing.** Reading, Mass.: Addison-Wesley, 1979.
31. Tavis, Alexander. "Concept Outline For Architectural Organization and Management: The Habitat Provision Process". unpublished course material, University of Illinois, Urbana, Illinois, 1977.
33. I. the concept of the Action Office.
34. Moore, Wilbert E. **Social Change.** Englewood Cliffs, N.J.: Prentice Hall, 1967.
35. Probst, Robert. Ibid.
36. Ibid.
37. Ibid.
38. Ibid.
39. Ibid.
40. Ibid.

41. Fuller, R. Buckminster. Ibid.
42. Bachelard, Gaston. **The Poetics of Space.** translated by Maria Jolas. New York: Orion Press, 1964.
43. Papanek, Victor. **Design for the Real World.** New York: Bantam, 1973.
44. Ibid.
45. Bloomer, Kent C. and Moore, Charles W. Ibid.
46. Op. Cit.
47. Katz, Jonathan G. "Images of Shiva". **Portfolio. Vol. III.** No. 3, May/June 1981, quotation of Dr. Stella Kramrisch, curator at the Philadelphia Museum of Art.
48. Singer, Jerome L. **Daydreaming.** New York: Random House, 1966.
49. Robertson, John Forbes. **Great Industries of Great Britain, II, 1886.** Diane Chalmers Johnson, "Louis Sullivan and American Art Noveau". **New Free Style: AD. Design Profile.** Ian Latham, editor, London: Architectural Design, 1980 quotation of John Forbes Robertson.
50. Fuller, R. Buckminster. Ibid.
51. The Rolling Stones.

THREE: PLACE

1. Fuller, R. Buckminster. **Utopia or Oblivion.** New York: Bantam, 1969.
2. Bloomer, Kent C. and Charles W. Moore. **Body, Memory and Architecture.** New Haven: Yale University Press, 1977.
3. Manuscripts by and discussions with Professor Robert Riley. Head - Department of Landscape Architecture, University of Illinois, Urbana-Champaign, 1977-1980.
4. Jackson, John Brinkerhoff. Conference presentation. "Renaissance Dream of the House," lecture at San Francisco Center for Architecture and Urban Studies Conference, **Making Dreams Come True: Design in the Aid of Fantasy.** February 5, 1981.
5. Clark, Sir Kenneth. **Civilization** the PBS Television series.
6. Bloomer, Kent C. and Charles W. Moore. **Body, Memory and Architecture.** New Haven: Yale University Press, 1977.
7. Jackson, John Brinkerhoff. Ibid.
8. Beeby, Thomas. Conference presentation, "Imagery of Taliesia," lecture at San Francisco Center for Architecture and Urban Studies Conference, **Making Dreams Come True: Design in the Aid of Fantasy.** February 5, 1981.
9. Manquel, Alberto and Guadalupi, Gianni. **The Dictionary of Imaginary Places.** New York: MacMillan, 1980.
10. Jackson, John Brinkerhoff. Ibid.
11. Johnson, Diane Chalmers. "Louis Sullivan and American Art Noveau". **New Free Style AD. Design Profile.** Ian Latham editor, London: Architectural Design. 1980.
12. Scully, Vincent J. **American Architecture and Urbanism.** New York: Praeger, 1969.
13. Op. Cit.
14. The Rookery Building was originally constructed to be the City Hall of Chicago. Before building an old water tower had to be removed from the site. This old structure had been a favorite roosting place for hundreds of city birds, hence they carried on to the new building as an appropriate label for the new roost of

lawyers and aldermen. The fascinating story of the rise of modern architecture from the ashes of the Chicago Fire is wonderfully told by Carl W. Condit in **The Chicago School of Architecture.** Chicago: The University of Chicago Press. 1964. Others interested in general urban or American studies will also enjoy **Chicago: Growth of a Metropolis** by Wade and Meyer. The Rookery still stands today (fortunately) as an office building and urban monument at the corner of LaSalle and Adams.

15. Johnson, Diane Chalmers. Ibid.
16. Ibid.
17. Ibid., quotation of Louis Sullivan, **Kindergarten Chats.**
18. Ibid.
19. Bing, Samuel. "L'Art Noveau". **New Free Style AD Design Profile.** Ian Latham editor, London: Architectural Design, 1980. Reprinted article from **Architectural Record. Vol. 12,** 1902.
20. Ibid.
21. Ibid.
22. Ibid.
23. Ibid.
24. Johnson, Diane Chalmers. Quotation from 'La premiere au Theatre de la Bourse, L' Etoile Belege, December 31, 1885.
25. Attributed to Louis Sullivan.
26. What sort of house does Carl Sagan live in anyway?.
27. Young, Mary Ellen. Conference presentation, "Buildings in Popular Fiction". **Making Dreams Come True: Design in Aid of Fantasy.** San Francisco Center for Architecture and Urban Studies, February 4, 1981.
28. Scully, Vincent J. **American Architecture and Urbanism.** New York: Praeger. 1969.
29. Johnson, Diane Chalmers. Ibid., quotation of Louis Sullivan **Kindergarten Chats.**
30. Ibid.
31. Mumford, Lewis. **The City in History.** New York: Harcourt, Brave & World, Inc. 1961.
32. Bacon, Edmund N. **Design of Cities.** New York: Penguin, 1976.
33. Ibid., quotation from his discussion of the ancient Panathenaic Procession "... from the Dipylon Gate at the city wall across Athens and up the slopes of the Acropolis..."
34. Scully, Vincent J. **Pueblo: Mountain, Village, Dance.** New York: The Viking Press, 1975. This latest book by this famous architectural critic/historian is his best expression of this principle between man's actions and his environments, which Scully has been exploring and developing throughout his important career.
35. Krier, Rob. "Typological and Morphological Elements of the Concept of Urban Space". **AD Design Profiles 18.** London: Architectural Design. Krier crusades for urban space for suit people. See also Camillo Sitte **The Art of Building Cities.** New York: Reinhold, 1945.
36. This is the natural process of urban renewal. The economics of the situation, means things: Property is less expensive because it s not as densely occupied (ie highly demanded) as land in the heart of the CBD. There are also more vacant areas providing flexible opportunities. Property values in transition areas can also be depressed by general negative characteristics of seedy neighborhoods — buildings in disrepair and questionable characters floating around. The state of semi-ruin can become part of the romantic charm of these places. Labor and material costs translate into tremendous savings if even only the principle structure and shell or a building are reused while all core and finish elements replaced. Sometimes it is even economically desireable to save the shell alone, or even just the front facade.

– NOTES

37. Riley, Robert. "The New American Landscape". unpublished manuscript. Urbana, Illinois, 1979.
38. Hoyt, Charles. "Building Types Study: Office Buildings in the Suburbs" **Architectural Record**. 10/74.
39. Appleyard, Donald, Lynch, Kevin and John R. Myer. **The View From the Road**. Cambridge: MIT Press, 1964.
40. American fold song.
41. My personal favorite wilderness retreat is a large tent on a raised wooden platform. The tents have roll up sides all the way around for a wonderful sense of openess. A 10'X15' space seems extra spacious under the high ridge of the pitched gable tent roof.
42. Jackson, John Brinkerhoff. **The Necessity of Ruins and other topics**. Amherst: University of Massachusetts Press, 1980.
43. Willie Nelson.
44. Filler, Martin. "Perfectly Frank". **Progressive Architecture**. July 1979.
45. Tsu, Lao. **Tao Te Ching**. translated by Gia-Fu Feng and Jane English. New York: Random House, 1972. Originally written in 6th century B.C.
46. Ching, Francis D.K. **Architecture: Form, Space & Order**. New York: Van Hostrand Reinhold Company 1979. Since the beginning of time, the upright marker such as a stone, or wooden totem pole have signified places special or even sacred. The tradition has been carried on in the art of fine painting and sculpture. Trajan's column as an acessory or code symbol for a very special place in fantastic or visionary works. The artist Radovich recently created a series of environmental sculptural pieces in which a columnar element energizes a sacred space.
47. Tyng, Ann. "The Geometric Extensions of Consciousness." In this article, Tyng describes the set of Platonic solids and their associations in ancient times: cube (earth), pyramid (fire), octahedran (air), icosahedron (water), and dodecahedron (cosmos). These solids were considered Platonic, that is, ideal because all sides were identical and their organization was completely regular. Ann Tyng is a practicing architect and a former associate of the late Louis I. Kahn.
48. Ibid.
49. Stravinsky, Igor. **Poetics of Music: In the Form of Six Lessons**. Cambridge: Harvard University Press, 1970.
50. Goethe.
51. Dave King, an unusual poet, treated his friends to a solo performance of his original opera, "Death of Sophocles" which he delivered from a shower, accompanying himself with "a chorus of Mack Trucks." His favorite motto, from Saunier's **Modern Horology** (c. mid-1800s): "Freedom is essential." Dave used to personalize his room by hanging door knobs and miscellaneous metal objects over his bed.
52. A famous saying from Ancient Greece which was 'rediscovered' during the Renaissance.
53. According to Sir Kenneth Clark, this is the principle illusion of western thought.
54. Marlin, William. "Two Business Buildings". **Architectural Record**. February, 1976.
55. Ibid.
56. For a detailed account of this development see Carl W. Condit's **The Chicago School of Architecture: A History of Commercial and Public Building in the Chicago Area 1875-1925**. Chicago: University of Chicago Press, 1964.
57. Krasnow, Iris. "Arthur the Magnificent", **Chicago**, April, 1981.
58. The first parrallelogram shaped office building is nearing completion of construction in South Bend; the First Bank Center by Murphy/Jahn of Chicago.
59. Marlin, William. "The New Energy Sources". **Architectural Record**. October, 1979.

60. The favorite adjective of a well-known Chicago architect who has designed many office buildings.
61. This problem is made even worse by the lack of good public transportation systems in smaller cities and towns.
62. Palladio, Andrea. **The Four Books of Architecture.** New York: Dover, 1965, first published in Venice, 1570. Palladio prescribed rooms of best proportion, length to width as follows: circle, square, 1:2, 3:4, 2:3, 3:5, 1:2. Height room usually equal to width.
63. McLuhan, T.C. editor. **Touch the Earth — A Self Portrait of Indian Existence.** New York: Promontory Press, 1971, quotation of the visionary, Black Elk.
64. Morton, David. "Chicago Traditions". **Progressive Architecture.** July, 1979.
65. Hoyt, Charles. "Building Types Study: Office Buildings in the Suburbs" **Architectural Record.** October, 1974.
66. Attributed to Janis Joplin.
67. Silvetti, Jorge. "The Beauty of Shadows", **Oppositions 9.** New York: Institute for Architecture and Urban Studies, Summer 1977.
68. Payne, Ifan. conference presentation, "Design for Fantasy in Art", **Making Dreams Come True: Design in Aid of Fantasy.** San Francisco Center for Architecture and Urban Studies, February 4, 1981.
69. Op. Cit.
70. Kinser, Bill and Neil Kleinman. **The Dream That Was No More A Dream.** Cambridge: Schenkman, 1969.
71. Payne, Ifan. Ibid.
72. Silvetti, Jorge. Ibid. quotation of Barthes.
73. Silvetti, Jorge. Ibid.
74. Bloomer, Kent C. and Charles W. Moore, Ibid.
75. Radovich, Zorine. PhD abstract of the aesthetics of being.

EPILOGUE

1. Kinser, Bill, and Kleinman, Neil. **The Dream That Was No More A Dream.** Cambridge: Schenkman, 1969.
2. Ibid.
3. Boaz.
4. Sagan, Carl. **Cosmos.** New York: Random House, 1980.
5. Scully, Vincent J. **Pueblo Mountain, Village, Dance.** New York: Viking Press, 1975.
6. Jefferson Airplane.
7. Stravinsky, Igor. **Poetics of Music: In the Form of Six Lessons.** Cambridge: Harvard University Press, 1970.
8. Williams, A. Richard, **The Urban Stage,** 1981.

BIBLIOGRAPHY

A.I.A. **Energy Conservation Design Guidelines For New Office Buildings.** Washington: GSA, 1975.

Agrest, Diana. "**Architectural Anagrams: The Symbolic Performance of Skyscrapers**", **Oppositions II.** New York: Institute for Architecture and Urban Studies, Winter 1977.

Aiken, Henry D. **The Age of Ideology: The Nineteenth Century Philosophers.** New York: Mentor, 1956.

Appleyard, Donald; Lynch, Kevin; John R. Myer **The View From The Road.** Cambridge: MIT Press, 1964.

Attoe, Wayne. **Architecture and Critical Imagination.** Chichester, New York: Wiley, 1978.

Bachelard, Gaston. **The Poetics of Reverie; Childhood, Language and the Cosmos.** New York: Orion Press, 1964.

Baldridge, Letitia. **Amy Vanderbilt's Complete Book of Etiquette: a guide to comtemporary living.** Revised and expanded. Garden City, New York: Doubleday, 1978.

Bacon, Edmund N. **Design of Cities.** New York: Penguin, 1976.

Banham, Reyner. **Theory and Design in the First Machine Age.** New York: Praeger, 1967.

Blaser, Werner. **Mies van der Rohe.** New York: Praeger, 1972.

Bloomer, Kent C. and Charles W. Moore. **Body, Memory, Architecture.** New Haven: Yale University Press, 1977.

Cage, John. **A Year From Monday.** Middletown, Connecticut: Wesleyan University Press, 1963.

Carpenter, Edmund. **They Became What They Beheld.** New York: Ballantine, 1970.

Ching, Francis D. K. **Architecture: Form, Space & Order.** New York: Van Hostrand Reinhold Company, 1979.

Christiansson, Carl. **The Office: How to Plan for Human Beings.** Unpublished manuscript. Stockholm, Sweden, 1977.

Clark, Sir Kenneth. **Leonardo da Vinci.** New York: Penguin, 1959.

Condit, Carl W. **The Chicago School of Architecture: A History of Commercial and Public Building in the Chicago Area 1875-1925.** Chicago: The University of Chicago Press, 1964.

Deilmann, Harald; Brickenbach, G. and Thomas. **Buildings for Banking and Insurance.** Germany: Kramer, 1978.

Flippo, Chet. "Checking in with Joseph Heller", **Rolling Stone.** April 16, 1981.

Fracchia, Charles A. **So this is where you work!: A guide to unconventional working environments.** Harmondsworth, England & New York: Penguin, 1979.

Fuller, R. Buckminster. **Utopia or Oblivion.** New York: Bantam, 1969.

Hitchcock, Henry-Russell and Philip Johnson. **The International Style.** New York: Norton, 1966.

Hitchcock, Henry-Russel. **Architecture: Nineteenth and Twentieth Centuries.** Baltimore: Penguin, 1971.

Hoyt, Charles King. **Buildings for Commerce and Industry.** New York: McGraw-Hill, 1978.

Jackson, John Brinkerhoff. **The Necessity for Ruins and Other Topics.** Amherst: University of Massachusetts Press, 1980.

Janson, H.W. **History of Art.** Englewood Cliffs, N.J.: Prentice-Hall, 1969.

Jaynes, Julian. **The Origins of Consciousness in the Breakdown of the Bicameral Mind.** Princeton: Princeton University Press, 1976.

Jones, Owen. **The Grammar of Ornament.** London: Bernard Quaritch, 1868.

Kandinsky, Vassily. **Concerning the Spiritual in Art.** Translated by M.T.H. Sadler. New York: Dover, 1977.

Originally published in 1914 in London by Constable, under the title **The Art of Spiritual Harmony.** Kieran, Stephen, editor. **Ornament: VIA III; Journal of the Graduate School of Fine Arts, University of Pennsylvania.** Philadelphia: Falcon Press, 1977.

Kinser, Bill and Neil Kleinman. **The Dream That Was No More A Dream.** Cambridge: Schenkman, 1969.

Koolhaas, Rem. **Delirious New York.** Oxford: Oxford University Press, 1978.

Kozinski, Jerzy. **Being There.** Krier, Rob. "Typological and Morphological Elements of the Concept of Urban Space", **A.D. Design Profiles 18.** London: Architectural Design.

Latham, Ian editor. **New Free Style, A.D. Design Profile.** London: Architectural Design, 1980.

Lao, Tsu. **Tao Te Ching.** Translated by Gia-Fu Feng and Jane English. New York: Random House, 1972. Originally written 6th Century B.C. in Honan province of China.

LeCorbusier. **Towards a New Architecture.** Translated by Frederick Etchells. New York: Praeger, 1960. Originally published in 1927 in London by Architectural Press.

Lethaby, William Richard. **Architecture, Mysticism, Myth.** New York: Braziller, 1975. Originally published in 1891 in London by Percival.

Manquel, Alberto and Gianni Guadalup. **The Dictionary of Imaginary Places.** New York: Macmillan, 1980.

Manasseh, Leonard and Roger Cunliffe. **Office Buildings.** New York: Reinhold, 1962.

McLuhan, T.C. editor. **Touch the Earth — A Self Portrait of Indian Existence.** New York: Promontory Press, 1971.

Meyer, Leonard B. **Music, The Arts And Ideas: Patterns and Predictions in Twentieth Century Culture.** Chicago: The University of Chicago Press, 1967.

Mills, Edward D. **The Changing Workplace: Modern Technology and the Working Environment.** London: George Godwin, Ltd., 1972.

Planning Buildings for Administration, Entertainment and Recreation. London: George Godwin, Ltd., 1976.

Planning Buildings for Habitation Commerce and Industry. London: George Godwin, Ltd., 1976.

Moore, Charles W. **Dimensions.** New York: McGraw-Hill, 1976.
Moore, Charles; Allen, Gerald; Lyndon, Donlyn. **The Place of Houses.** New York: Holt, Rinehart and Winston, 1974.
Moore, Wilbert E. **Social Change.** Englewood Cliffs, New Jersey: Prentice-Hall, 1967.
Mumford, Lewis. **The City in History.** New York: Harcourt Brace & World, 1961.
Norberg-Schulz, Christian. **Existence, Space and Architecture.** New York: Praeger, 1971.
Ouchi, William. **Theory Z.** Reading, Massachusetts: Addison-Wesley, 1981.
Owens, Bill. **Suburbia.** San Francisco: Straight Arrow Books, 1973.
Palladio, Andrea. **The Four Books of Architecture.** New York: Dover, 1965. First published in Venice, circa 1570.
Papanek, Victor. **Design for the Real World.** New York: Bantam, 1973.
Pederson, Eldor Olin. **Office Location.** Monticello, Illinois: Council of Planning Librarians, 1977.
Pevsner, Nikolaus. **An Outline of European Architecture.** Baltimore: Penguin, 1943.
Piaget, Jean. **Origins of Intelligence in Children.** Translated by Margaret Cook. New York: International University Press, 1952.
Pile, John F. **Interiors Second Book of Offices.** New York: Whitney Library of Design, 1969.
Interiors Third Book of Offices. New York: Whitney Library of Design, 1976.
Open Office Planning: A Handbook for Interior Designers. New York: Whitney Library of Design, 1978.
Probst, Robert. **The Office — an organization based on change.** Ann Arbor, Michigan: Herman Miller, 1969.
Ram Dass, Baba. **Journey of Awakening.** New York: Bantam, 1978.
Rapoport, Amos. **House Form and Culture.** Englewood Cliffs, New Jersey: Prentice Hall, 1969.
Reinhold, Hohl. **Office Buildings: An International Survey.** New York: Praeger, 1968.
Riley, Robert. "The Landscape of Memory" and "The New American Landscape." Unpublished manuscripts, Urbana, Illinois, 1978.
Ripnen. **Office Building & Office Layout Planning.** New York: McGraw-Hill, 1960.
Office Space Administration. New York: McGraw-Hill, 1974.
Rosenfeld, Edward. **The Book of Highs.** New York: Quadrangle, 1973.
Rudofsky, Bernard. **Architecture Without Architects.** Garden City, New York: Doubleday, 1964.
Sagan, Carl. **Cosmos.** New York: Random House, 1980.
Scully, Vincent J. **American Architecture and Urbanism.** New York: Praeger, 1969.
The Earth, the Temple and the Gods: Greek Sacred Architecture. New York: Praeger, 1969.
Scully, Vincent J. **Frank Lloyd Wright.** New York: Braziller, 1960.
Louis I. Kahn. New York: Braziller, 1962.
Modern Architecture: The Architecture of Democracy. New York: Braziller, 1974.
Pueblo: Mountain, Village, Dance. New York: The Viking Press, 1975.
The Shingle Style Today Or, The Historian's Revenge. New York: Braziller, 1974.
Schmertz, Mildred. **Office Building Design.** New York: McGraw-Hill, 1975.

Shoshkes, Lila. **Space Planning: Designing the Office Environment.** New York: McGraw-Hill, 1976.

Silvetti, Jorge. "The Beauty of Shadows", **Oppositions 9.** New York: Institute for Architecture and Urban Studies, Summer 1977.

Singer, Jerome L. **Daydreaming.** New York: Random House, 1966.

Singer, Jerome L. and Kenneth S. Pope editors. **The Power of Human Imagination: New Methods in Psychotherapy.** New York: Plenum, 1978.

Sitte, Camillo. **The Art of Building Cities; City building according to its artistic fundamentals.** Translated by Charles T. Stewart. New York: Reinhold, 1945.

Sommer, Robert. **Personal Space; the behavior basis of design.** Englewood Cliffs, New Jersey: Prentice Hall, 1969.

Stravinsky, Igor. **Poetics of Music: In the Form of Six Lessons.** Cambridge: Harvard University Press, 1970.

Strunk, William Jr. and E.B. White. **The Elements of Style.** New York: MacMillan, 1979.

Sullivan, Louis H. **A System of Architectural Ornament According with a Philosophy of Man's Powers.** New York: N.Y. Times, 1966. Originally published in 1924 in New York by Eakins Press.

Tavis, Alexander. "Concept Outline For Architectural Organization and Management: The Habitat-Provision Process." Unpublished course material for Architecture 430, University of Illinois, Urbana, Illinois, 1977.

Terkel, Studs. **Working.** New York: Avon, 1974.

Thompson, J.D. **Organizations in Action.** New York: McGraw-Hill, 1967.

Toffler, Alvin. **The Third Wave.** New York: Bantam, 1980.

Tyng, Ann. "The Geometric Extensions of Consciousness." Venturi, Robert. **Complexity and Contradiction in Architecture.** New York:, MOMA 1966.

Venturi, Robert; Scott-Brown, Denise; Izenour, Steven. **Learning From Las Vegas.** Cambridge: MIT Press, 1972.

Wade, Richard C. and Harold Melvin Mayer. **Chicago: Growth of a Metropolis.** Chicago: University of Chicago Press, 1969.

Wallechinsky, David. **What Really Happened to the Class of 65?.**

Watts, Alan. **Beat Zen, Square Zen & Zen.** and **Does it Matter?.**

Weick, Karl E. **Social Psychology of Organizing.** Reading, Mass. Addison-Wesley, 1979.

White, Morton. **The Age of Analysis: 20th Century Philosophers.** New York: Mentor, 1955.

Williams, A. Richard. **The Urban Stage.** 1981.

Wolfflin, Heinrich. **Principles of Art History.** Translated by M.D. Hottinger. New York: Dover, 1950.